Science and Technology in India

Science and Technology in India

Developmental Profile

P. Satyanarayana
Lakshmi Mantha
C. Sesharatnam

SHIPRA

Rs. 995; US$ 39.80

ISBN: 978-93-88691-06-2

First Published in India in 2019

Science and Technology in India: Developmental Profile

Published by:
SHIPRA PUBLICATIONS
LG 18-19, Pankaj Central Market,
I.P. Ext., Patparganj, Delhi-110092, India
Tel.: +91 11 2223 5152/ 6152
E-mail: info@shiprapublication.com
www.shiprapublication.com

Contents

1
Before Independence

The impression that science started only in Europe was deeply embedded in the minds of educated people all over the world. Thanks to the work of the Indian National Science Academy and other learned bodies, the development of sciences in India during the ancient period has drawn attention of scholars in the 20th century. It is clear from the studies that India has consistently been a scientific country and right from Vedic to modern times—with the usual fluctuations that can be expected of any country. In fact we do not find an example, except perhaps that of ancient Greece, which accorded the rare exalted place to knowledge as did that of India.

Mathematics

Vedic Hindus evinced special interest in two particular branches of Mathematics, viz., Geometry and Astronomy. There is considerable material on Astronomy in Vedic Samhitas. But everything is shrouded in such mystic expressions and allegorical legends that it has now become extremely difficult to discuss their proper significance. However, much seems to have been made in the Brahmana period when Astronomy came to be regarded as a separate science called *Nakshatra Vidya*.

Astronomy

Scientific Indian Astronomy dates from the year A.D. 499 when Aryabhatta began to teach Astronomy to his pupils. Bhasakara, the direct pupil of Aryabhatta, narrated Aryabhatta's system of Astronomy.

Ayurveda

Ayurveda, the traditional system of medicine, is a special branch of knowledge on life dealing with the body and mind. Ayurveda is concerned with the origin of life and intelligence which are external. The history of Ayurveda may be divided into four stages—first, the beginning period; second, the period of complications; third, the period of epitomes; and finally fourth, the period of decline. These four periods are marked by three distinct types of Ayurvedic treaties.

The decline of Ayurveda began in the period of the *Sangrahas*, when medical authorities started summarising the classics and codifying them as separate treatises.

Engineering

The achievements of Indians in the field of engineering began in the proto-historic times, from the third millennium B.C. or even earlier. The ancient Indian civilisation like those of Iran, Iraq, Mesopotamian, Egypt showed skills in the construction of buildings and granaries, in town planning and with provision of civic amenities like community baths and other sanitary conveniences. The earliest evidence of the technical skills of the ancient Indian lies perhaps in the numerous tools he carved out of stone in the course of his struggle for existence.

Remains of the Indus Valley Civilisation (4th–3rd millennium B.C.) unearthed at Mohenjo-Daro and Harappa, Lothal and Kalibangan simply testify to the well developed technical skills of ancient Indians. Mohenjo-Daro and Harappa are deemed to have been the capital cities of Indus Valley. The dwellers of Mohenjo-Daro were among the world's pioneers in city construction. The houses unearthed are commodious and well built, indicating the civil engineering skill of the people. The Indus Valley people achieved proficiency in engineering and technical skills.

The Gupta period (A.D. 300–600) saw the beginning of systematic construction on the basis of structural principles in temple architecture from the 5th century A.D. Brick-built religious structures, both Buddhist and Brahmanical, gradually became common in the alluvial plains. These include Buddhist Chaitya halls, monasteries and stupas as well as Brahmanical temples. The post Gupta period witnessed brick buildings activity with experiment in various temple forms.

Medicine

Muslim rule started in India with the onset of 13th century A.D. and lasted for around five hundred years and concluded with the death of Aurangzeb in 1707. During this period, considerable work was done in various spheres of science and technology. Sciences such as mathematics, medicine, astrology, astronomy flourished. It is also true that in medieval India, science was not patronised as a state policy by Kings or Rajas. It is unfortunate that science technology was not pursued rigorously as it was being developed in Europe.

Monuments Construction

Huge monuments were constructed, observatories were built, texts were translated but the volume was too low in comparison with the west. Inspite of all these hurdles, science flourished in a scanty manner. The money that was spent on constructing monumental edifices, had it been spent on scientific institutions, India could have become an advanced country long time ago.

Significant Science and Technology Discoveries in Ancient India

Indian civilisation has a strong tradition of science and technology. Ancient India was a land of scholars and scientists. Research has shown that India was actively contributing to the field of science and technology centuries long before modern laboratories were set up. Many theories and techniques discovered by the ancient Indians have created and strengthened the fundamentals of modern science and technology. The following are some of the ground breaking contributions listed by Sanchari Pal.

1. *The Idea of Zero*

Little needs to be written about the mathematical digit 'zero', one of the most important inventions of all time. Mathematician Aryabhatta was the first person to create a symbol for zero and it was through his efforts that mathematical operations like addition and subtraction started using the digit zero. The concept of zero and its integration into place-value system also enabled one to write numbers, no matter how large, by using only ten symbols.

2. *The Decimal System*

India gave the ingenious method of expressing all numbers by means of ten symbols—the decimal system—each symbol received a value of position as well as an absolute value. Due to the simplicity of the decimal notations which facilitated calculation, this system made the uses of Arithmetic in practical inventions much faster and easier.

3. *Fibonacci Numbers*

The Fibonacci numbers and their sequence first appear in Indian Mathematics as *Matrameru*, mentioned by Pingala in connection with the Sanskrit tradition of prosody (the study of poetic metres and verses). Later on, the methods for the formation of these numbers were given by Mathematicians Virahankar, Gopala and Hemachandra, much before the Italian mathematician Fibonacci introduced the fascinating sequence to Western European Mathematics.

Binary numbers is the basic language in which computer programmes are written. Binary basically refers to a set of two numbers, 1 and 0, the combinations of which are called bits and bytes. The binary number system was first described by the Vedic scholar Pingala, in his book *Chandhahsastra* which is the earliest known Sanskrit treatise on prosody.

4. Chakravala Method of Algorithms

The chakravala method is a cyclic algorithm to solve indeterminate quadratic equations, including the Peil's equation. This method for obtaining integer solutions was developed by Brahmagupta, one of the well known mathematicians of the 7th century CE. Another mathematician, Jayadeva later generalised this method for a wider range of equations, which was further refined by Bhaskara II in his *Bijaganita* treatise.

5. Ruler Measurements

Excavations at Harappan sites have yielded rulers or linear measures made from ivory and shell. Marked out in minute subdivisions with amazing accuracy, the calibrations correspond closely with the *hasta* increments of 1 3/8 inches, traditionally used in the ancient architecture of South India. Ancient bricks found at the excavation sites have dimensions that correspond to the units on these rulers.

6. A Theory of Atom

One of the notable scientists of the ancient India was Kanad who is said to have devised the atomic theory centuries before John Dalton was born. He speculated the existence of *anu* or a small indestructible particle, much like an atom. He also stated that *anu* can have two states—absolute rest and a state of motion. He further held that atoms of same substance combined with each other in a specific and synchronised manner to produce *dvyanuka* (diatomic molecules) and tryanuka (triatomic molecules).

7. The Heliocentric Theory

Mathematicians of ancient India often applied their mathematical knowledge to make accurate astronomical predictions. The most significant among them was Aryabhatta whose book, *Arybhatiya* represented the pinnacle of astronomical knowledge at the time. He correctly propounded that the Earth is round, rotates on its own axis and revolves around the Sun, i.e. the heliocentric theory. He also made predications about the solar and lunar eclipses, duration of the day as well as the distance between the Earth and the Moon.

A pioneering steel alloy matrix developed in India, Wootz steel, characterised by a pattern of ands that was known in the ancient world by many different names such as Ukku, Hindwani and Seric Iron. This steel was used to make the famed Damascus swords of yore that could cleave a free-falling silk scarf or a block of wood with the same ease. Produced by the Tamils of the Chera Dynasty, the finest steel of the ancient world was made by heating black magnetite ore in the presence of carbon in a sealed clay crucible kept inside a charcoal furnace.

8. *Smelting of Zinc*

India was the first to smelt zinc by the distillation process, an advanced technique derived from a long experience of ancient alchemy. The ancient Persians had also attempted to reduce zinc oxide in an open furnace but had failed. Zawar in the Tiri valley of Rajasthan is the world's first known ancient zinc smelting site. The distillation technique of zinc production goes back to the 12th Century A.D. and is an important contribution of India to the world of science.

9. *Seamless Metal Globe*

Considered one of the most remarkable feats in metallurgy, the first seamless celestial globe was made in Kashmir by Ali Kashmiri ibn Luqman in the reign of the Emperor Akbar. In a major feat in metallurgy, Mughal metallurgists pioneered the method of lost-wax casting to make twenty other globe masterpieces in the reign of the Mughal Empire. Before these globes were rediscovered in the 1980s, modern metallurgists believed that it was technically impossible to produce metal globes without any seams, even with modern technology.

10. *Plastic Surgery*

Written by Sushruta in 6th Century B.C., *Sushruta Samhita* is considered to be one of the most comprehensive textbooks on ancient surgery. The text mentions various illnesses, plants, preparations and cures along with complex techniques of plastic surgery. The *Sushruta Samhita's* most well-known contribution to plastic surgery is the reconstruction of the nose, known also as rhinoplasty.

11. *Cataract Surgery*

The first cataract surgery is said to have been performed by the ancient Indian physician Sushruta way back in 6th century BCE. To remove the cataract from the eyes, he used a curved needle, Jabamukhi Salaka, to loosen the lens and push the cataract out of the field of vision. The eye would then bandaged for a few days till it healed completely. Sushruta's surgical works were later translated to Arabic language and through the Arabs, his works were introduced to the West.

12. *Ayurveda*

Long before the birth of Hippocrates, Charaka authored a foundational text, *Charakasamhita,* on the ancient science of Ayurveda. Referred to as Father of Indian Medicine, Charaka was the first physician to present the concept of digestion, metabolism and immunity in his book. Charaka's ancient manual on preventive medicine remained a standard work on the subject for two millennia and was translated into many foreign languages, including Arabic and Latin.

13. Iron-Cased Rockets

The first iron-cased rockets were developed in the 1780s by Tipu Sultan of Mysore who successfully used these rockets against the larger forces of the British East India Company during the Anglo-Mysore Wars. He crafted long iron tubes, filled them with gunpowder and fastened them to bamboo poles to create the predecessor of the modern rocket. With a range of about two kilometres, these rockets were the best in the world at that time and caused as much fear and confusion as damage. Due to them, the British suffered one of their worst ever defeats in India at the hands of Tipu.

Beginning of Modern Science and Technology

The British brought to India contemporary science and technology—what is often termed as 'modern' science and technology. However, the educational/research developments in this period were directed to meet the British Government's needs, and not primarily meant for India's socio-economic betterment. But, unwittingly, perhaps, these activities promoted indigenous efforts to develop scientific thought.

The foundation of the Asiatic Society in 1784 by Sir William Jones marked the beginning of public interest in scientific research. The Society helped the founding of the Indian Museum of Calcutta in 1866. The Asiatic Society published papers in physics, chemistry, geology and medical sciences, and thus played an important role in the advancement of sciences in India.

The Indian Association for the Cultivation of Science, founded in 1876 by Dr. Mahendralal Sarkar, provided laboratory facilities and became a prominent scientific research centre in the country. One may also recall the Bombay Natural History Society, founded in 1883, and the Indian Mathematical Society, which was started in 1907 mainly through the efforts of V. Rangaswami Iyer under the name of Analytical Club with its headquarters at Fergusson College, Poona.

The Calcutta Mathematical Society was established in 1908 with Sri Ashutosh Mukhopadhyay as its first president, with the objects of fostering and encouraging the study of Mathematics in all its branches, promoting the spirit of original research, and publishing a periodical.

The efforts of Prof. P.S. MacMohan of Lucknow and Prof. Simon of Madras led to the formation of the Indian Science Congress Association in 1914. The establishment of this society played a major role in creating a scientific consciousness bringing scientists together and enabling them to make the government give support to scientific research.

The main scientific activities in the Government sector were largely carried out by the medical and the engineering corps of the army and civil officers interested in science, as a spare time activity. These men, trained in European institutions and laboratories, left a record of their work and made a mark in various branches of sciences through original contributions.

They brought out considerable literature on science and technology built up a sizable store of scientific apparatus, chemicals and research tools, and founded a few of the important scientific institutions in the country. They created a tradition of dedicated scientific research, and the Indians who worked under them carried this forward.

Geologists had been employed since 1818 for survey work. In 1851, the Geological Survey of India was organised, under the efforts of Thomas Oldham, the then Professor of Geology in Dublin. The beginning of geological studies may be traced to last quarter of the 18th century. A series of discoveries of Siwalik fossils—and research on these—were made by H. Falconer and P.T. Cautlay.

The Trigonometrical Survey of the Peninsula of India was established in 1800 and was expanded as Great Trigonometrical Survey of India in 1818. The Topographical and Revenue Surveys grouped together under the Surveyor General of India in 1817 and a School of Surveying established in Madras, after several transformations, were consolidated with Trigonometrical Survey in 1878 as the survey of India.

The Botanical Gardens were established in 1788. Dr. William Roxbery was the first to start research on Indian plants in the Botanical Gardens. The Botanical Survey of India was established in 1890. Zoological research in India dates back to the appointment of Edward Blyth as the Curator of the Museum of the Asiatic Society in 1814. His successor, John Anderson, became in 1866 the Superintendent of the Indian Museum with the zoological and anthropological collections under his direct charge. In 1916, the zoological and anthropological sections of the Indian Museum were converted into the Zoological Survey of India.

Significantly enough, while those areas of science and technology which served British industrial interests were developed early. Industrial research and needs of industry were not given much attention by the British, as they wished to keep India as a supplier of raw material to British industries and a market for British manufactures.

The requirements of the First World War and the political pressure of the national movement, however, led to the appointment of the Holland Commission in 1918 for appraising, amongst other things, the status of the then existing industrial research facilities, and to make recommendations for its improvement.

Nothing much was done till 1935 when the Government established an Industrial Intelligence and Research Bureau with the object of "making a beginning and to lay the foundation on which a research organisation suitable for the needs of the country could later be constructed". An Industrial Research Council was set up to advice on measures for the coordination and development of industrial research.

Once again, the Second World War forced the then Government to establish units to serve the needs of a besieged Britain. The Board of Scientific and Industrial Research was established to advise the government on research for development of Indian industries, particularly those connected with the war. The Board emphasised the need and provided the basis for a central organisation to plan research, to bring about effective coordination to the research activities in the country, and to promote the application of research for national development.

In 1942, an Industrial Research Fund was created by the Government for the purposes of fostering industrial development in the country, and the Council of Scientific and Industrial Research (CSIR) was constituted as an autonomous body to administer the fund.

The proposals for the establishment of a National Physical Laboratory and a National Chemical Laboratory were accepted, and plans for other laboratories for food technology, building, road, leather, electro chemicals and others were later formulated.

These plans were taken up after independence and research institutes were established for these areas, incidentally on the lines of the institutes established in the United Kingdom, under the Department of Scientific and Industrial Research.

It was the high incidence of diseases unknown to the West, the cost of their treatment, and their impact on army and administration that necessitated research in British-ruled India relating to diseases like cholera, plague, malaria, beri-beri, *kala azar*, etc. In 1892, the Bacteriological Laboratory at Agra was established with P.H. Hankin as its head.

The spread of plague in Bombay in 1896 led to the deputation of W.M. Haffkine to work on this problem. In 1899, Haffkine developed a plague vaccine and established a small laboratory, called Plague Research Laboratory, in Bombay (renamed in 1926 as Haffkine Institute). The Pasteur Institute was established at Kasauli in 1900. Three years later, the King Institute was established at Guindy for the manufacture of calf-lymph and for general bacteriological work.

In 1907, another Pasteur Institute was set up at Coonoor. In 1910, Sir Leonard Rogers proposed the establishment of the School of Tropical Medicine in Calcutta. Thus, a chain of institutes with facilities for medical research was established and a cadre of scientific workers in the field created.

Sir Harcourt Butler, first Member of the Department of Education, Health and Lands, of the Viceroy's Executive Council, and Sir Pardy Lukis, the Director-General of Indian Medical Service, worked towards the establishment of an Indian Research Fund Association in 1911. Its primary objectives being research, propagation of knowledge and experimental measures generally in connection with the causation, mode of spread and prevention of communicable diseases.

Agricultural research began with the establishment of the Agricultural Research Station and Experimental Farm (later called the Imperial Institute of Agricultural Research) at Pusa in Bihar with the help of a donation by an American philanthropist, Henry Phipps of Chicago. Subsequently, separate departments of agriculture were constituted in different provinces.

Agricultural colleges were established at Ponna, Kanpur, Nagpur, Layallpur (now in Pakistan), Coimbatore and Sabour. In 1921, agriculture, which had so far been a central subject, was transferred to provinces, which were to deal with policy, administration, coordination of agricultural research and education.

A Royal Commission on Agriculture was appointed in 1926 to examine and report on condition of agriculture and the rural economy of India with particular reference to the measures being taken for the promotion of agriculture and veterinary research and education. Its recommendations led to the establishment of the Imperial Council of Agricultural Research in 1929 with the primary object of promoting, guiding and coordinating agricultural research and education in India.

The Council was also to serve as a link between agricultural institutions in India and in foreign countries. A number of central commodity committees dealing with research in particular crops, namely cotton (1921), jute (1936), sugarcane (1944), tobacco (1945), coconut (1945), and oilseeds (1947), were also set up as semi-autonomous bodies.

A bacteriological laboratory was established in 1889 in Pune, subsequently transferred to Mukteshwar in 1893. The branch at Izatnagar, Bareilly, was opened in 1913 and the name changed to Imperial Veterinary Institute (now known as Indian Veterinary Research Institute).

Not much research activity was carried on in private institutes. A few institutes were established by scientists or public men, some of them being the Indian Institute of Science, Bangalore (1911); the Bose Institute, Calcutta (1917), the Indian Academy of Science, Bangalore (1934) of which the Raman Research Institute is a part; Sheila Dhar Institute of Soil Sciences, Allahabad (1936); the Tata Institute of Fundamental Research, Bombay (1945); Shri Ram Institute for Industrial Research, Delhi (1947).

Institutes like the Indian Institute of Science, Bangalore, established by the Tatas, played a notable role as a centre of research at a time when India possessed few research facilities. Their development was accelerated only after Independence and they are now centres of higher studies and research in their respective fields.

Though the policy of promotion of science and technology and their use for developing agriculture, health and industry was guided by political considerations, a number of dedicated British scientists found in India unlimited possibilities for contributing to knowledge. Their research and collection of valuable data did much for building a modern scientific base for the country.

Their deliberations, new standards of objectivity, and respect for facts as a part of discussions created a new awareness amongst the people, made them realise the importance of science and technology and the possibilities of development through their use. Scientific and technological infrastructure, once created, begins to interact with situations and opportunities, and helps in promoting a self-generating scientific and technological tradition.

The political leadership of the Independence movement continuously brought pressure on the then government for greater educational facilities and creation of industries. As a result, when India became free it had, in contrast to many other colonies, a scientific and technological foundation which would support the future needs of a newly independent country, provided the political leadership was visionary enough to utilise it.

2
After Independence

In India there has been a long and distinct tradition of scientific research and technological advancement since ancient times. Since independence, we have accelerated our speed and efforts in this field and have established many research laboratories, institutions of higher learning and technical education. The results have been such as would make anybody's heart swell with pride, confidence and a sense of fulfillment. The best, however, is yet to come.

The central and state governments, various public and private sector establishments are engaged in scientific research and technological development to take the nation on the path of rapid development, growth and prosperity. There are about 200 research laboratories spread all over the country. The institutions of higher learning, and universities, the modern temples of learning, are all committed to take the country forward. They are well equipped and staffed to secure for the people of the nation all the blessings and benefits that can accrue from the acquisition and application of scientific knowledge and technology. But there is no room for complacency, for in this field only the sky is the limit and we are yet a developing country.

Our technology policy is comprehensive and well thought out. It aims at developing indigenous technology to ensure efficient absorption and adoption of imported technology suitable to national priorities and availability of resources. Its main objective is attainment of technical competence and self-reliance, leading to reduction in vulnerability in strategic and critical areas. With a view to strengthening our economy and industrial development, our government has introduced many structural reforms through adoption of a new industrial policy which has an important bearing on the programmes of development pertaining to science and technology. Consequently, technology has become our mainstay enterprise and now we have built a strong and reliable infrastructure for research, training and development in science and technology.

In the field of agriculture, our scientific and technological researches have enabled us to be self-reliant and self-sufficient in food grains. Today, we can withstand droughts and natural calamities with much greater confidence than ever before. Now, we are in a position to export food grains, etc. and are on the threshold of white and blue revolutions. Thanks to our agricultural scientists and farmers, always ready to imbibe new technologies, we have many varieties of hybrid seeds, crop-protection technologies, balanced farming practices and better water and irrigation management techniques. Similarly in the field of industrial research, we have achieved many milestones and India is emerging as a major industrial power of the world. The Council of Scientific and Industrial Research (CSIR), with its network of research laboratories and institutions, has been chiefly instrumental in our major achievements in scientific and industrial research. We have now joined the exclusive club of six advanced nations by developing our own super computer at the Centre for Development of Advance Computing (C-DAC) at Pune.

Our Atomic Research Commission, set up in 1948, is engaged in valuable nuclear research for peaceful purposes. The executive agency for implementing atomic energy programmes is the Department of Atomic Energy. The Bhabha Atomic Research Centre, Trombay, near Mumbai is the biggest single scientific establishment in the country, directing nuclear research. Now, we have five research reactors, including Apsara, Cirus, Dhruva, Zerlina and Purnima. We have carried out two underground nuclear tests at Pokhran in Rajasthan. This is a remarkable achievement by our nuclear scientists, which has enabled us to become one of the selected few countries of the world to have done it. India is also the first developing country, and one of the seven countries in the world to master fast breeding technology. Research in breeder technology is currently going on at Indira Gandhi Centre for Atomic Research at Kalpakkam, Chennai.

The successful launching of Polar Space Launching Vehicle (PSLV-D-2), in October 1994, marked India's entry into the league of the world's major space powers. In the INSAT-2 series of satellites, launched first in 1992, India has shown its ability to fabricate complex systems comparable to anything made anywhere in the world. Our previous launches of the SLV-3 and the SLV were merely stepping stones to what will be the workhorses of the business, the PSLV, which can launch one tonne satellite into orbit of up to 1000 km, and the Geosynchronous Satellite Launch Vehicle (GSLV), which can take 2.5 tonne satellite to orbits 36,000 km away. India's space programme rocketed to greater heights with the successful launch of the second Geosynchronous Satellite Launch Vehicle (GSLV-D2) in May, 2003. As has been rightly observed, the challenge before Indian Space Research Organisation (ISRO) is to maintain the momentum of the programme by integrating it with other missions. The most obvious ones are related to military communication and reconnaissance.

Our success on Antarctica speaks volumes of our scientific genius and technological wisdom in the field. So far, 13 scientific expeditions by our oceanographers, scientists and technicians have been to Antarctica and we have two permanent stations on the icy continent.

In the field of defence also our achievements have been quite laudable. The successful production of such missiles as Prithvi and Nag testify to the high capabilities and achievements of our scientists. We have also been successful in producing opt-electronic fire control and night-vision devices required for our indigenous tanks. The HAL at Bengaluru has already produced Advanced Light Helicopter (ALH).

Obviously, technology has been used effectively as a tool and instrument of national development and yet much remains to be achieved in order to make its benefits reach the masses. Scientists in the country will have to strive hard to take technological developments to people's doorsteps.

Modern India has had a strong focus on science and technology, realising that it is a key element of economic growth.

India is among the topmost countries in the world in the field of scientific research, positioned as one of the top five nations in the field of space exploration.

The expansion of scientific contemplation in modern India can be credited to the scientists of the nineteenth century.

They essentially shaped the way we live now and many of the scientific research work currently in progress follows the lead of these brilliant thinkers.

The inception of modern science in India and its passage has left its lasting imprint for the posterity to dwell upon the subsequent proliferation of science.

Indian scientists were not given the credits of discoveries which were passed on to British officers even if they didn't have anything to do with the discovery.

Scientific fingerprinting was born in India but the laurels were heaped on others, the naming of Everest was not justified among many such other instances.

The India's Independence in 1947 brought the urge to explore, indigenise and also usher in modern science and nurture sophisticated technologies.

And now India's detection of gravitational waves opens up new frontier for understanding of universe.

During the period of Independence, Particle physics in India was highly developed and the world recognition followed.

Bose-Einstein collaboration and findings of Meghnad Saha are some exemplary instances.

The study of natural sciences is on full swing.

The Botanical Society of India and Zoological Society of India came forward with the unchartered flora and fauna of the planet. Paleobotany flourished under Birbal Sahni.

The Geological Survey of India and the Survey of India had laid its modicum of research areas that later bore results at the hands of people like D.N. Wadia and Radhanath Sikdar respectively.

Meghnad Saha ushered in stellar astrophysics. He started the physics department in Allahabad University and Institute of Nuclear Physics, National Academy of Science in 1930, Indian Physical Society in 1934 and the Indian Institute of Science in 1935, Saha Institute of Nuclear Physics in 1943, and the Indian Association for the Cultivation of Science in Kolkata. Saha was also the chief architect of river planning in India. He made the original plan for Damodar Valley Project.

C.V. Raman excelled in astrophysics while working at the Indian Association of Cultivation of Science, the cornerstone of modem science in India founded in the earlier century by Mahendralal Sarkar.

S.N. Bose became an advisor to the newly formed Council of Scientific and Industrial Research (CSIR). He was the president of Indian Physical Society and the National Institute of Science.

CSIR has been ranked 12th in the world, amongst the government institutions, improving its position after being at the 14th position for three consecutive years, with an overall global ranking of 99 in the world during 2016, according to the report of Scimago Institutions Rankings.

On an average, CSIR files about 250 Indian patents and 300 foreign patents per year.

About 13 per cent of CSIR patents are licensed, that remains above the global average.

The indelible ink used during the General Elections in India was developed by CSIR in 1952. This innovation of CSIR is now exported to more than 25 countries including Canada, Turkey and South Africa.

Subsequently, the Indian Institutes of Technology came up in Kharagpur in 1951 and charted a seminal course of Indian research and technology.

Indian Arctic programme started in 2008 with the setting up of Indian research base, Himadri. In 2012, India became a member of the International Arctic Science Committee and in 2013, India was accorded permanent observer state in the Arctic Council. So far, there have been 42 expeditions, five exams per year. In 1981, Indian scientists had reached the Antarctic and set up Bharati station. India's first moored observatory was deployed in the Arctic.

In 2015, India became a part of International Ocean Drilling Programme in the Arabian Sea.

Science without Humanity [is sin], maintained Gandhiji.

One apt instance of science benefiting livelihood is the Potential Fishing Zone Services for all 14 sectors of the Indian coastline. It has increased the net profit of fishermen by 3-4 times in the range of 34,000 to 50,000 crore. From one village of 32 fishing boats, there is diesel saving of 70,000 litres per month. 40 per cent users are small craft fisher folk who have witnessed an average increase of Rs. 16,000 in their income when fishing in Potential Fishing Zones.

Earthquake monitoring, cyclone predictions and Tsunami Warning System are safeguards against vagaries of nature.

The 21st century in India is apparently marked as the beginning towards an advancement in terms of technology and enrichment of knowledge base in the field of Science.

At present, India holds a strong position in terms of advanced technology. India also serves as a knowledge warehouse with the existence of its many institutions catering to Science and Technology which come with qualified and trained manpower.

The different areas which undergo development with the advancement in Science and Technology are:

- Higher education
- Scientific research and development
- Technological development
- Advancement of agricultural system
- Development of space science and technology
- Development of medical science and technology
- Development of infrastructure
- Information and communication technology
- Development of various fields of engineering (including software, chemical, mechanical, civil, electrical, electronic, etc.)

Likewise, India has strong scientific and technological base that spreads across the country in the form of academic institutions, research and development laboratories, advanced medical centre (with research facilities), experimental centres, and different advanced industries.

Because of the development in all spheres of science and technology, today India is unquestionably a leading developing country in the world.

Over the recent past, science and technology has made tremendous contribution towards the settlement of industries in India.

Starting from the micro level to the macro level, research and development in the field of technology has created an ideal niche for the overall growth of the economic condition of the country. The perceptible examples are the development of Atomic Energy, Space Science, dozens of successful satellite systems, advanced medical technologies, etc.

After the independence, it was not possible for India to depend on other countries for various aspects of development; therefore, the development of indigenous technology was indispensable for the overall development of a country.

Thankfully, today, Indian technologies and companies are as competent as in other developed countries. India is also a lead in various fields, and is a tough competitor for other countries.

If we discuss about the skilled human resources, many Indians are at top-notch positions in leading companies.

Indian industries started flourishing post 1990, i.e., the landmark era. Globalisation, liberalisation and privatisation facilitated this growth. The industries catering to Information and Technology, Atomic Energy, Automotive, Biotechnology, Nanotechnology, Pharmaceutical, Petroleum, etc. have increased at global level.

On the other hand, the Government of India has also made sizable investment in the field of research and development to encourage the advancement of Indian economy.

For consistent and efficient growth, various initiatives have been taken by establishing the following organisations:

- Council of Scientific and Industrial Research (CSIR)
- Department of Science and Technology (DST)
- All India Institute of Medical Sciences (AIIMS)
- Aryabhatta Research Institute of Observational Sciences (ARIES)
- Central Drug Research Institute (CDRI)
- Centre for the Study of Developing Societies (CSDS)
- Central Electronics Engineering Research Institute (CEERI)
- Central Food Technological Research Institute (CFTRI)
- Central Glass and Ceramic Research Institute (CGCRI)
- Central Institute of Agricultural Engineering (CIAE)
- Central Institute of Brackish water Aquaculture (CIBA)
- Central Soil Salinity Research Institute (CSSRI)
- Indian Institute of Engineering Science and Technology (IIEST)
- Indira Gandhi Centre for Atomic Research (IGCAR)
- Institute of Economic Growth
- Institute of Genomics and Integrative Biology (IGIB)
- National Institute of Electronics and Information Technology (NIELIT)
- National Institute of Pharmaceutical Education and Research (NIPER)
- National Institute of Oceanography (NIO)

Likewise, there are dozens of other such scientific research centres which have been set up for the overall economic growth of the country.

Science and Technology and Society in India

The growth, peace, and security of a society is directly related to the development of the technology; as Science and Technology in a way influences the development as well as security of the society.

Consider the following points to understand how the security of a society is directly related to the development of the technology.

- CCTV Camera at various locations (especially at public places) is one of the best examples of keeping crime under surveillance and it also provides a sense of security to the people.
- Because of the advancement in technology, today, there is a reduction in communication gap; people have the information of where their near and dear ones are and are just a phone call away at times of need.
- The job of the police has become easier, as police can trace criminals easily.
- Besides, because of the advancement of technology, today, most of the villages in India have electricity, road, and can avail for essential facilities.
- People, who are residing in even very remote part of the country, have the benefit of entertaining themselves and upgrading their knowledge through the different programmes broadcast on television (with dozens of channels).
- Telecommunications network towers have been set up at the remotest of the remote regions too.

Some Significant Achievements

Several Indian government agencies promote and develop science and technology in the country. Some of such organisations are:

1. Department of Scientific and Industrial Research (DSIR)
2. Council of Scientific and Industrial Research (CSIR)
3. Indian Council of Agricultural Research (ICAR)
4. Indian Council of Medical Research (ICMR)

1. Salient Achievements of Department of Scientific and Industrial Research, New Delhi

(I) Industrial R&D Promotion Programme (IRDPP): This is one of the flagship schemes of DSIR which has supported in providing recognition and registration to about 1,800 in-house R&D units of the companies and 1,200 Scientific and Industrial Research Organisation (SIRO's) and Public Funded Research Institution (PFRI's) so far. The institutes and industry

recognised by DSIR can claim for income tax relief on R&D expenditure, customs and excise duty exemption, weighted tax deduction u/s 35 (2AB) of the IT Act 1961. The incentive of 200 per cent weighted tax deduction is one of the best in the world and provides for incentivising the R&D sentiments of the industry to attain global competitiveness. The department at present is providing fiscal incentives to over 1,000 companies for claiming weighted tax deduction u/s 35 (2AB) of IT Act 1961. The department has submitted reports valued at around Rs. 10,000 crore to the Director General of Income Tax (Exemptions) during the FY 2015-16 to enable the industry claim weighted tax deduction u/s 35(2AB) of IT Act 1961. The foregone revenue due to several tax exemptions and concessions has been increasing over the years but has significantly contributed to the R&D and innovation in the industry.

(II) Technopreneur Promotion Programme (TePP): This is an erstwhile scheme of DSIR and has been one of the most creative schemes for promoting individual innovator, grass-root innovator by providing grant-in-aid support to them for converting their ideas into economically viable products/processes. DSIR has supported more than 600 individual innovators and more than 30 TePP outreach centres. Several success stories have been created and awarded patent. Some of these are:

(i) Development of pollution free technology for starch processing plants;
(ii) Development of extendable width cultivator which is workable with higher horse power tractors and the futile need of purchasing the matching implement is avoided;
(iii) Production of filler grade PTFE, which will reduce plastic waste and help in minimising ecological problems;
(iv) Development of a cost-effective method for synthesising and processing nano crystalline hydroxyapatite (HAP), a bioactive and bio-compatible material used as bone substitute material and in drug delivery systems. This innovation will enable the orthopedic surgeries become affordable even by the common masses;
(v) Development of wet and dry scrubbers as pollution control devices for diesel-vehicles, tractors and DG sets upto 15 KVA.

(*Source*: Report prepared by Department of Scientific and Industrial Research (DSIR) on Creative India, Technopreneur Promotion Programme (TePP, 2010).

Some of the other completed projects during the year 2013-14 are:

(i) Development of portable, non-invasive oral cancer detection system;

(ii) Low cost multi-media projector;
(iii) Supportive limb for physically challenged; and
(iv) Mrityunjay—an advanced electronic distant patient monitoring system.

(III) Promoting Innovations in Individuals, Start-ups and MSMEs (PRISM): It is a newly formulated scheme and some of the ongoing projects under the scheme are: (i) automated garment dyeing, chemical washing and effluent treatment wet processing machine for cotton textiles and cotton garments; (ii) Low cost sequence embroidery machine for zari and zardosi work; (iii) Development of pesticide mixer cum sprayer agricultural pump which is operable by single person and will replace traditional system of spraying in orchids, crop and vegetable fields. The accuracy in the ratio of water to pesticides is also maintained.

(IV) Patent Acquisition and Collaborative Research and Technology Development (PACE): It is also a newly formulated scheme under the 12th plan and supports projects for technology development and demonstration in the industry and some of the projects that have been supported are the following:

(i) Technological upgradation of steam sterilisation based palletisation facility for development of microbe free, her balveterinary supplement for the benefit of livestock such as poultry, aqua ruminants, etc. which are a part of the food chain.
(ii) Macro algal Bio-refinery for CO2 sequestration and production of bio-fuel and value added compounds for economic sustainability.
(iii) Chitosan based drug delivery system for dental and oral diseases.
(iv) Development of genetically engineered cellulose for alkaline xylanase through submerged fermentation process (SMF). Due to the inconsistency in the yield of the product, the company had opted for recombinant route for expressing the geneviz. Bacillus pumilusin Pischia pastoris, a well studied host used in the production of recombinant enzymes.

(V) Access to Knowledge for technology Development and Dissemination (A2K): The scheme is supporting: (i) Technology Development and Utilisation Programme for women for creating awareness and training of women for promotion and adoption of new technologies; (ii) Technology Development and Demonstration Programme (TDDP), which is operational since 1992 and the department has supported more than 250 projects with a total project cost of Rs. 750.60 crore in which the DSIR support had been about Rs. 280 crore. Seventy six technologies developed under the TDDP scheme have been commercialised and the department

has earned a cumulative royalty of around Rs. 33 crore. Some of the technologies that have been commercialised are: (i) Digital axle counter for railway signalling (ii) PC based CNC system; (iii) Development of micro balance of 200 gm capacity with 1 mg accuracy; (iv) Glargine process improvement; (v) Development of an interactive multimedia package for intellectual property rights training.

2. Salient Achievements of Council of Scientific and Industrial Research, New Delhi

1. (i) CSIR through NMITLI scheme has been successful in developing a reflectance confocal microscope and has paved the way for photonics research in India. This is one of the best examples of "Made in India", high end product.

   (ii) CSIR under the NMITLI scheme, with a focused effort to develop sustainable energy solutions has endeavoured to develop indigenous know-how and technology for building proton exchange membrane fuel cell (PEMFC) multi cell stack of desired power output, which has also been validated for commercial application and use as telecom tower power backup. The modular test bed for validation has been designed, built and commissioned with in-house know-how at Reliance Industries Limited, Patalgangasite.

2. (i) The National Aerospace Laboratory (NAL), Bangalore is a proud associate with Indian Space Research Organisation (ISRO) in India's first reusable Launch Vehicle–Technology Demonstration (RLV-TD). The acoustic test on RLV-TD was carried out at the Acoustic Test Facility of CSIR, NAL during April 2016.

   (ii) The National Aerospace Laboratory (NAL) has also developed spectrally selective coatings for solar thermal power generation and application. The know-how for the development of technology for commercial production of absorber coatings is available with NAL.

   (iii) The National Aerospace Laboratory (NAL) and the Indian Meteorological Department (IMD), are jointly producing the Drishti system, which is an indigenous hi-tech visibility system to manage takeoff and landing at airports under conditions of lowest visibility of 50 metres. Till now, only seven airports in the country have been armed with the Drishti visibility system and mega project of installing such 70 systems across the country's various airports is under way.

   (iv) The Aeronautical Development Agency (ADA) and Department of Defence R&D is the nodal agency for the design and development of Light Combat Aircraft, Tejas. Hindustan Aeronautics Limited (HAL) was the principal partner in LCA programme with participation of Defence Research Development Organisation (DRDO) and CSIR laboratories, public and private sector industries. National Aerospace Laboratory (NAL) has spearheaded the team effort to design, develop and certify the fly-by wire flight control laws and air data algorithm for Tejas.

3. The Central Scientific Instruments Organisation (CSIO), Chandigarh, has developed an earthquake warning system (EQWS) which records the events and generates SMS to the concerned action point in real time. Recently CSIO using this (EQWS) has alerted the Delhi Metro about the 6.8 magnitude of the earth quake recorded in Hindukush region of Afghanistan on 10 April 2016.
4. National Botanical Research Institute, Lucknow, has developed low arsenic rice grain. The new variety has "arsenic methyl transferase gene", isolated from a fungus that accumulates less arsenic and would be less toxic. The variety is almost ready for field trials.
5. CSIR, with Department of Science and Technology has developed the first Indian Gyrotron (a device used in nuclear fusion process and which is presently imported in the country) and is ready to be tested at the Institute of Plasma Research, (Department of Atomic Energy), Gandhinagar, which is a partner institute of the project.
6. CSIR-Indian Institute of Petroleum, Dehradun has developed and transferred the technology for making a catalyst that will reduce Sulphur in LPG.
7. CSIR and Oil and Natural Gas Corporation Ltd. (ONGC) has established a unique PPP mode for exploration of natural resources for oil and gas from ONGC oil fields in Krishna-Godavari basin.
8. (i) CSIR-Central Mechanical Engineering Research Institute (CMERI) has developed a 10 hp tractor named Krishi Shakti which is cost effective (Rs. One lakh) and is suitable for small and marginal farmers. CMERI had done the nation proud when in 1970 it first designed and developed the 20 hp Swaraj tractor, the first indigenous tractor of the country. Thereafter, CMERI designed the 35 hp Sonalika tractor, which has gone into major production.

   (ii) CMERI has also developed Soleckshaw (Solar-Electric Rickshaw). It is an eco-friendly mode of urban transport system which is dual powered and driven partly by pedal and partly by electric power supplied battery that is charged from solar energy. The technology has been commercialised to some of the companies.

9. National Physical Laboratory (NPL), New Delhi developed the chemical composition of the indelible ink which is used as an electoral ink and the process involved in the manufacturing of the ink is licensed and is a closely guarded secret.
10. Central Food Technological Research Institute (CFTRI), Mysore, in the late 1950's developed a process for the production of infant food from buffalo's milk. The technology was licensed to the Kaira District milk producers union at Anand, Gujarat, which produced infant food under the brand name Amulspray and which soon became a popular household name. The product has also been distributed under the special nutrition programme, Integrated Child Development Service Scheme (ICDS), run by the various state Governments.
11. Institute of Microbial Technology (IMTECH), Chandigarh has designed a new-generation clotbuster protein streptokinase and the know-how for the production has been licenced to Nostrum Pharmaceuticals Inc., USA about a decade ago. The primate studies for toxicological safety and efficacy have been successfully completed, validating the proof-of-concept of this molecule.

3. Salient Achievements of Indian Council of Agricultural Research, New Delhi

Indian Council of Agricultural Research has a vast network of research institutes, national research centres and bureaus, state agriculture universities and is a pioneer organisation responsible for sustainable food-grain production in India with major milestones being achieved as green revolution (food grains), white revolution (milk), yellow revolution (oilseeds), blue revolution (fish) and golden revolution (fruits and vegetables). The research and development efforts of the organisation have enabled the increase in production of food grains by five times, horticultural crops by more than nine times, fish by more than 12 times and milk by around eight times in the last 60 years. Some of the remarkable achievements of ICAR are enumerated below:

(i) Developed and released nearly 3,300 high-yielding varieties/hybrids of field crops for different agro-ecological zones.

(ii) Developed single cross hybrids in Quality Protein Maize (QPM) and baby corn for high nutritional value in addition to high yield.

(iii) Agriculturally important micro-organisms, plant growth promoting rhizo-bacterium (PGPR), Bacillus amyloliquefaciens

IISR GRB 35 has been bio-encapsulated for smart delivery in crops. The patent for the invention has also been filed.

(iv) Developed the bio insecticide strain DOR Bt-l, registered and commercialised its formulation KNOCK W.P. along with a low-cost mass multiplication methodology for integrated management of semi looper caterpillar in a number of crops; developed endosulfan-tolerantstrain of Trichogramma chilonis (Endo-grama); deployed Pest Management Information System including Interactive Kiosks for Basmati rice, cotton, mustard, chickpea and groundnut.

(v) Prepared soil resource maps of the country (1:1 million scale), states (1:250,000 scale) and 55 districts (1: 50,000 scale); soil degradation map of the country (1: 4.4 million scale) and state soil erosion maps (1:250,000 scale).

(vi) Developed a portable soil test kit/mini lab (Mridaparikshak) to supplement soil testing service in the country. The kit is useful in analysing soil samples for the purpose of distributing soil health cards to farmers.

(vii) Developed liquid bio fertilizer formulations with longer shelf life. Identified potassium and zinc solubilising bacteria and standardised vermin/ bio-enriched composting technology.

(viii) Indian Agricultural Research Institute has developed an indigenous semi-synthetic super absorbent polymer "Pusa Hydrogel" which has a remarkable ability to reduce irrigation/ fertigation requirement of crops besides improving crop yield and quality under restricted or limited irrigation conditions. The bench scale technology has been licensed to six companies.

(ix) National Research Centre on Plant Biotechnology (NRCPB) has developed transgenic brinjal with a Bt gene (cry1Fa1), which is very effective against BSFB.

(x) National Research Centre on Plant Biotechnology has also developed transgenic tomato (Pusa Ruby) with cry1Ac gene for protection against the fruit borer. The Bt-tomato was tested with promising results and licensed in 2011 to a private company for bio safety testing and commercialisation under Public-Private Partnership.

(xi) NRCPB has developed a high yielding mustard variety, named, 'Pusa Jai Kisan' through tissue culture technique, called soma clonal variation. The popular commercially released variety, Varuna (Type 59) was used as a donor parent for generating somaclonal variation.

4. Salient Achievements of Indian Council of Medical Research (ICMR), New Delhi

ICMR promotes biomedical research in the country through in tramural research (by its own institutes/centres) and extramural research (through grants-in-aid given to projects to non-ICMR institutes). ICMR is working under the Department of Health Research (DHR) and has a country wide network with more than 30 institutes. Some of the major milestones achieved by ICMR in the field of affordable diagnostics, therapeutics-drugs and devices/treatment methods and vaccines are enumerated below:

- (i) Indigenous technologies for the following have been developed and launched: (a) Japanese Encephalitis vaccine (JENVAC) under public private partnership with Bharat Biotech India Pvt. Ltd., Hyderabad; (b) Thalassemia detection kit developed by National Institute of Immunohaemotology, Mumbai; (c) An "AV Magnivisualiser" for detection of cervical cancer developed by Institute of Cytology and Preventive Oncology (ICPO), Noida; (d) PCR based food pathogen detection kit, ELISA kit for Ferritin estimation and Dried Blood Spot (DBS) collection kit for vitamin A analysis, all developed by the National Institute of Nutrition, Hyderabad, (*Source*: Indian Council of Medical Research, Annual Report 2013-14).
- (ii) The National Institute of Virology (NIV), Pune completed the restructuring of Virus Repository at par with international protocols of bio security and standards. The activity has been successfully launched as a part of the NIV Bio Banking programme and viruses given to researchers in the country.
- (iii) Regional Medical Research Centre, Port Blair has worked for the development of DNA vaccine against leptospirosis. The DNA vaccine construct based on LipL45 sequence elicited both cell mediated and humoral immune response in experimental animals and the Centre is providing referral services in leptospirosis to various institutions in the country as well as to neighbouring countries. Diagnostic services (Microscopic Agglutination Test performance) was provided to 11 centres, leptospiral reference strains were supplied to 22 centres and control sera to three centres.
- (iv) Technology on Vijaysar, an antidiabetic drug generated in 1999 has been sold to a company after signing a tripartite agreement and assignment deed between the Indian Institute of Integrative Medicine (IIIM), Jammu and ICMR. This technology was an outcome of the joint effort of Indian Institute of Integrative Medicine (IIIM), Jammu (CSIR) and ICMR.

(v) Enterovirus Research Centre, Mumbai has contributed significantly to the understanding of epidemiology of poliomyelitis and developing polio vaccination strategies in India and the most significant achievement of the Centre has been the achievement of "zero polio" status in India.

(vi) The Desert Medicine Research Centre (DMRC), Jodhpur has developed herbal composition against larvae of dengue vectors which can be used as an effective and sustainable bio-larvicide to check vector breeding and eliminate virus foci possibly circulating through vertical transmission.

3
National Policies

India has a long and distinguished tradition in science and technology from the ancient times. The great achievements during the last century, the latter half prior to independence, have been related largely to pure research. At the time of independence, our scientific and technological infrastructure was neither strong nor organised as compared to the developed world. This had resulted in our being technologically dependent on the skills and expertise available in other countries. There is now a reservoir of expertise well acquainted with the most modern advances in basic and applied areas that is equipped to make choices between available technologies, to absorb readily new technologies and provide a framework for future national development.

Department of Science and Technology (DST) was established in May 1971, with the objective of promoting new areas of Science and Technology and to play the role of a nodal department for organising, coordinating and promoting S&T activities in the country. The Department has major responsibilities for specific projects and programmes as listed below:

1. Formulation of policies relating to Science and Technology.
2. Promotion of new areas of Science and Technology with special emphasis on emerging areas.
3. Futurology.
4. Coordination and integration of areas of Science and Technology having cross-sectoral linkages in which a number of institutions and departments have interest and capabilities.
5. Undertaking or financially sponsoring scientific and technological surveys, research design and development, where necessary.
6. Support and Grants-in-aid to Scientific Research Institutions, Scientific Associations and Bodies.
7. All matters concerning:

(a) Science and Engineering Research Council;
(b) Technology Development Board and related Acts;
(c) National Council for Science and Technology Communication;
(d) National Science and Technology Entrepreneurship Development Board;
(e) International Science and Technology Cooperation;
(f) Autonomous Institutions relating to the subject under the Department of Science and Technology including Institute of Astro-physics, and Institute of Geo-magnetism;
(g) Professional Science Academies funded by Department of Science and Technology;
(h) The Survey of India, and National Atlas and Thematic Mapping Organisation;
(i) National Spatial Data Infrastructure.

8. Matters commonly affecting Scientific and technological departments/organisations/ institutions, e.g. financial, personnel, purchase and import policies and practices.
9. Management Information Systems for Science and Technology and coordination thereof.
10. Matters regarding Inter-Agency/Inter-Departmental coordination for evolving science and technology missions.
11. Matters concerning domestic technology particularly the promotion of ventures involving the commercialisation of such technology other than those under the Department of Scientific and Industrial Research.
12. All other measures needed for the promotion of science and technology and their application to the development and security of the nation.
13. Matters relating to institutional Science and Technology capacity building including setting up of new institutions and institutional infrastructure.
14. Promotion of Science and Technology at the State, District, and Village levels for grass- roots development through State Science and Technology Councils and other mechanisms.
15. Application of Science and Technology for weaker sections, women and other disadvantaged sections of Society.

National Policies

1. Science Policy Resolution, 1958
2. Technology Policy Statement, 1983

3. Science and Technology Policy, 2003
4. Science, Technology and Innovation Policy, 2013

Changing Phases of National Policies in S&T

India's Scientific Policy Resolution (SPR) of 1958 resolved to "foster, promote and sustain" the "cultivation of science and scientific research in all its aspects". Technology was then expected to flow from the country's established science infrastructure. The Technology Policy Statement (TPS) of 1983 emphasised the need to attain technological competence and self-reliance. The Science and Technology Policy (STP) of 2003 brought science and technology (S&T) together and emphasised the need for investment in R&D. It called for integrating programmes of socio-economic sectors with the national R&D system to address national problems as well as creating a national innovation system.

Need for a Science, Technology and Innovation Policy

Scientific research utilises money to generate knowledge and, by providing solutions, innovation converts knowledge into wealth and/or value. Innovation thus implies S&T-based solutions that are successfully deployed in the economy or the society. It has assumed centre stage in the developmental goals of nations. Paradigms of innovation have become country and context specific. India has, hitherto not accorded due importance to innovation as an instrument of policy. The national S&T enterprise must now embrace S&T led innovation as a driver for development.

India has declared 2010-20 as the "Decade of Innovation". The Government has stressed the need to enunciate a policy to synergise science, technology and innovation and has also established the National Innovation Council (NInC). The STI Policy 2013 is in furtherance of these pronouncements. It aims to bring fresh perspectives to bear on innovation in the Indian context.

Science, Technology and Innovation (STI) Policy: A New Paradigm

Science, technology and innovation can exist separately on their own in disconnected spaces. But, it is their integration that leads to new value creation. India's global competitiveness will be determined by the extent to which the STI enterprise contributes social good and/or economic wealth. There is, therefore, the need to create the necessary framework for enabling this integration in identified priority areas by exploiting endogenous resources, strengths and capacities. New structural mechanisms and models are needed to address the pressing challenges of energy and environment, food and nutrition, water and sanitation, habitat, affordable health care and skill building and unemployment. "Science technology and innovation for the people" is the new paradigm of the Indian STI enterprise. The national STI system must, therefore, recognise the Indian society as its major stake holder. Global innovation systems tend to bypass large sections of the community. Innovation for inclusive Growth implies ensuring access, availability and affordability of solutions to as large a population as possible. Innovation, therefore, must be inclusive. The instruments of the STI policy will enable this to be realised. The policy will drive both investments in science and investment of science-led technology and innovation in select areas of socio-economic importance. Emphasis will be to bridge the gaps between the STI system and the socio-economic sectors by developing a symbiotic relationship with economic and other policies.

Capturing Aspirations

The key elements of the STI policy are:

- Promoting the spread of scientific temper amongst all sections of society.
- Enhancing skill for applications of science among the young from all social strata.
- Making careers in science, research and innovation attractive enough for talented and bright minds.
- Establishing world class infrastructure for R&D for gaining global leadership in some select frontier areas of science.
- Positioning India among the top five global scientific powers by 2020.
- Linking contributions of science, research and innovation system with the inclusive economic growth agenda and combining priorities of excellence and relevance.
- Creating an environment for enhanced Private Sector Participation in R&D.
- Enabling conversion of R&D outputs into societal and commercial applications by replicating hitherto successful models as well as establishing of new PPP structures.
- Seeding S&T-based high-risk innovations through new mechanisms.
- Fostering resource-optimised, cost-effective innovations across size and technology domains.

- Triggering changes in the mind-set and value systems to recognise, respect and reward performances which create wealth from S&T derived knowledge.
- Creating a robust national innovation system.

Attracting Private Sector Investments in R&D

Public funds for partnerships with the private sector for social and public good objectives will be earmarked as a new policy initiative. A National Science, Technology and Innovation Foundation will be established as a Public-Private Partnership (PPP) initiative for investing critical levels of resources in innovative and ambitious projects.

The focus of the policy will be:

- Facilitating private sector investment in R&D centres in India and overseas.
- Promoting establishment of large R&D facilities in PPP mode with provisions for benefits sharing.
- Permitting multi stakeholders participation in the Indian R&D system.
- Treating R&D in the private sector at par with public institutions for availing public funds.
- Bench marking of R&D funding mechanisms and patterns globally.
- Modifying IPR policy to provide for marching rights for social good when supported by public funds and for co-sharing IPRs generated under PPP.
- Launching newer mechanisms for nurturing Technology Business Incubators (TBIs) and science-led entrepreneurship.
- Providing incentives for commercialisation of innovations with focus on green manufacturing.

Public Awareness and Public Accountability of Indian STI Sector

Public understanding of science is an important dimension for introducing and reaching the benefits of modern science and technology to the people. The civilisational aspect of science, or scientific temper, needs to be promoted across all sections of the society systematically. Effective science communication methods, by using tools such as the National Knowledge Network, will be initiated.

Public and political understanding of science should be based on evidence and debates with open mind. People and decision makers must be made aware of the implications of emerging technologies, including their ethical, social and economic dimensions. White papers on mission-oriented programmes, with specific deliverables and timelines, will be published. Mechanisms for assessing the performance of the national STI enterprise through an autonomous and robust evaluation system, which includes social scientists, will be established. The national science academies will be accorded a major role in this endeavour of public accountability.

Policy Vision

The guiding vision of aspiring Indian STI enterprise is to accelerate the pace of discovery and delivery of science-led solutions for faster, sustainable and inclusive growth. A strong and viable Science, Research and Innovation System for High Technology-led path for India (SRISHTI) is the goal of the new STI policy.

4

Five-Year Plans

The aim of five-year planning in India had been an overall development but as far as planning is concerned with science and technology, the aim was to foster, promote and sustain the cultivation of the sciences and scientific research and to encourage individuals for dissemination of scientific knowledge and above all to secure all benefits that accrue from the acquisition and application of scientific knowledge for the people of the country.

However, India has developed its own model of R&D planning. The planning process adopted over the years is a two way process involving brood policy guidelines from the Planning Commission and ensuring interaction with scientists at national, agency laboratory and university levels. This ensures the effective participation of the scientific community in decision-making. The planning process involves the following steps:

(i) The government declares its policy guidelines and thrust areas which are communicated to research agencies and institutions.
(ii) Specialised branches of science, areas of research and development are asked to prepare plans in respective areas.
(iii) These plans are coordinated at laboratory level and discussed by scientific advisory panels of respective laboratories.
(iv) These plans at laboratory level are coordinated at agency level and scrutinised by experts. But the final scrutiny is done at the planning commission level and finalised, and then resources are allocated.

However, the First Plan aimed at the setting up of new national laboratories and research institutes, training the personnel for manning the research institutes and running industries. The translating the results of scientific research into commercial production, the exploration and survey of resources were also emphasised.

During the Second Plan, efforts were made to strengthen research facilities, coordinating research programmes in various national laboratories and institutions with the need of national plan, linking up research work at the national level with the regional and state level. This plan also focused to train and generates scientific manpower in sufficient numbers and ensuring its proper utilisation. The linking of research and industrial need was also emphasised.

The Third Plan emphasised to strengthen the existing research institutes and expand facilities for research in engineering and technology with a view to developing industrial and manufacturing instruments.

The fourth plan laid emphasis on purposeful research and development programmes and the priority areas identified under the plan were steel, chemicals instruments, etc. The cooperation of outside agencies other than the CSIR also sought in the plan. The plan also aimed at avoiding duplication of research work of different laboratories and stressed on the utilisation of indigenous expertise and materials in the nuclear power projects. Space department also got proper attention.

The fifth plan attempted to restructure the research programme into projects with predetermined time spans, cost and benefits. In agriculture special emphasis on programmes to control crop diseases, dry farming and agricultural implements, surveying and research of natural resources.

The sixth plan included the task of creating a scientific temper for growth of science and its utilisation in developmental process. A close nexus between science, and technology and space was envisaged. The plan also aimed to create new research institution in the field of plasma physics, immunology and applied microbiology.

The Seventh plan emphasised on policies and programmes to accelerate the growth in food production and to raise its productivity. It recognised emergence on world scene, such as micro-electronics, informatics, telemetric, robotics, biotechnology, material science, instrumentation, etc.

The eighth plan sought to integrate science and technology with socio-economic sectors and more particularly rural areas to meet the basic needs of water, nutrition, health and sanitation, shelter, energy, education and employment. The plan also emphasised to set up sophisticated infrastructure, instrumentation and trained man power.

The tenth plan was given out to New Science and Technology Policy 2003, in order to build a blue print for future programmes of science and technology. The policy outlines the approach to S&T governance, optional utilisation of existing physical and knowledge sources, development of innovative technologies, system and technologies for mitigation and management of natural hazards, generation and management of intellectual property and creation of awareness among general masses about the use and benefits of science and technology.

Realising the need to invest heavily to bring development in science and technology and to meet the goals set under Vision 2025, the Eleventh Five-Year Plan endorsed by National Development Council has tripled the proposed allocation for scientific research and development. In order to boost the research and development activities in the country, the government has enhanced the S&T plan outlays for Scientific Departments and Agencies from Rs. 25,243 crore in the tenth plan to Rs. 73,304 crores for the eleventh plan.

Further various initiatives have been proposed by the government to encourage investment on Research and Development both in the institutions and industry through served measures such as—setting up of new institutions for science education and research, creation for centres of excellence, strengthening infrastructure for research and development in universities and encouraging public-private partnership in research and development.

The plan also envisages the formulation of a National Innovation Policy to encourage competition among enterprises, greater diffusion of knowledge. It also talks of putting in place a legislative framework for providing incentives to investors.

It has also proposed for the establishment of Centres of Relevance and Excellence (CORE) in academic and Research and Development institutions in selected areas that are relevant to industries.

Other proposals include the Council for Advancement of People's Action and Rural Technology (CAPART) to become an effective link between technology generation centres and various ministries for dissemination and propagation of technology packages through employment generation and capacity building schemes. Apart from it creations of biotech clusters in Delhi, Gujarat, Haryana, Orissa, Punjab and West Bengal have been proposed.

National Biotechnology Regulatory Authority for single window clearance for all biotechnological products was proposed. Besides these thirty Central Universities, eight new IITs, seven IIMs, ten new National Institute of Technology and three Indian Institute of Science Education and Research were proposed during the Eleventh Five-Year Plan.

5
Infrastructure Creation

After independence, in the year 1974, the Government of India consciously sought the development of science and technology as a major force for measuring in social and economic changes.

A Scientific Policy Resolution was enabled in March 1958, by the Government of India, which became the magna cart for the development of science in modern India. The main aim of the policy was to foster, promote and sustain the cultivation of science and scientific research in all aspects and in general to secure for people of the country all the benefits that can accrue from the acquisition and application of scientific knowledge.

Twenty five years later a technology Policy Statement was introduced in 1983, which emphasised the need to attain technological competence and self-reliance. The basic objective of the Policy was the development of indigenous technology and efficient absorption and adaptation of imported technology appropriate to national priorities and resources. The 2013 Policy focuses on "Shaping the Future of an Aspiring India". The National Innovation Council was setup. It aimed to bring fresh perspectives to bear as innovation in the Indian context. The National Innovation Foundation was also setup. The 2013 STI Policy covered the following:

- Investment in Research and Development (R&D)
- Promoting Excellence and Relevance in R&D
- Participating in Global R&D Infrastructure and Big Science
- Performance Linked Rewards and Investments
- National Agenda and the STI system
- Attracting Private Sector Investment in R&D
- Delivery System for STI outputs to stake Holders and Society

Recognising the importance of science and technology as a major force in industrial and economic growth, the visionaries led to the creation of scientific and technological infrastructure in India:

- The zeal of Sir (Dr.) Shanti Swarup Bhatnagar led to the establishment of CSIR (Council of Scientific and Industrial Research) and formation of a chain of national R&D laboratories spanning over a wide spectrum of science, technology, engineering and biomedical sciences.

- The vision of Prof. Homi Jehangir Bhabha led to advanced research in nuclear energy and other fundamental areas through the creation of Tata Institute of Fundamental Research and the entire gamut of activities coming today under the aegis Atomic Energy Commission.
- The Space programme envisioned by Dr. Vikram Sarabhai in the seventies has grown into a self-confident and dynamic era of the space science in India.
- Prof. D.S. Kothari provided a new thrust to the development of R&D programmes for defence, as well as to plan modern technical education system in the country.
- While Prof. R.C. Mahalanobis provided blue print on the role of science in economic planning. The attempt was to achieve rapid economic growth in a manner in which political and economic democracy would be reconciled by using modern scientific approaches.

The modern science in India has been nurtured by the individual initiatives, as well as by the government encouragement and political support. India in the process of building capacities and capabilities in science and technology in the country and has created a sizeable institutional infrastructure base in education, S&T and industry. Various scientific departments, R&D organisations/ labs and technical institutions have been established in the country for performing R&D activities, developing S&T manpower, determining and deploying instruments and carrying out other ancillary work. There is a chain of R&D laboratories, established under the:

- Council of Scientific and Industrial Research (CSIR),
- Indian Council of Agricultural Research (ICAR),
- Indian Council of Medical Research (ICMR), and
- Defence Research and Development Organisation (DRDO).

Say about 50 national level R&D laboratories (each) and 80 regional centers, covering a wide spectrum of botanical plants to aerospace engineering, totaling about 4000 S&T institutions.

The Government of India has created several full-fledged subject oriented scientific ministries to provide greater push to these scientific subjects respectively and to develop them completely towards global progress. A Ministry of Science and Technology, was created in 1985 with three scientific departments under it i.e. Department of Scientific and Industrial Research (DSIR), Department of Biotechnology, as well as Department of Science and Technology. But, the Ministry of Science and Technology is a truncated one and has no jurisdiction over the other subject-oriented scientific ministries. An apex science Advisory Council to the then Prime Minister (Rajiv Gandhi) during 1986-90 recommended the setting up of a National Commission for Science and Technology to over-see the "functioning", their provision of budget, coordination of R&D work, prioritisation of S&T activities vis-à-vis socio-economic needs, inter-ministerial linkages, etc. of all the Scientific Departments, has been overlooked.

S&T Infrastructure Establishment (Select)

Important S&T Infrastructure in India

1948 Department of Industrial Development
1950 National Flaming Commission
1951 Ministry of Scientific Research and Natural Resources
1953 University Grants Commission
1954 Department of Atomic Energy
1958 Defence Research and Development Organisation
1961 National Council of Educational Research and Training
1961 National Research Development Corporation of India
1961 National Industrial Development Corporation
1961 Engineers India Limited
1969 Indian Space Research Organisation
1970 Department of Electronics (Now Ministry of Electronics and Information Technology) (MeitY)
1971 Department of Science and Technology (DST)
1972 Department of Space
1980 Department of Environment (now Ministry of Environment, Forests and Climate Change)
1981 Department of Ocean Development
1982 Department of Non-conventional Energy Sources (now Ministry of New and Renewable Energy)
1984 Department of Bio-Technology (DBT)
1984 Department of Scientific and Industrial Research (DSIR)
1986 Ministry of Science and Technology (with DST, DBT and DSIR)
1987 National Institute of Immunology
2005 Ministry of Earth Science
2015 NITI Aayog (in place of Planning Commission)

Atomic Energy

The year 1948 was a milestone in India: An Atomic Energy Commission was set up on 15 August 1948 while an Atomic Energy Act of 15 April 1948 (revised in 1962, 1982, 1987 and 2015) gave a concrete shape to the atomic energy development in the country. The Government of India recognised, way back in the 1950's, that Nuclear Energy offered a tremendous potential for the economic development especially for a developing country like India. The highlights are:

1974 India conducted first Nuclear Test at Pokhran-I on 18 May 1974. Nuclear Suppliers Group (NSG), slapped sanctions on India. Nuclear winter begins.

1968 India refuses to sign Nuclear Non-Proliferation Treaty (NPT), on the grounds that it is discriminatory.

1998 India conducted five Nuclear tests on 11 May and 13 May 1998, at Pokhran-II, declares India to be a nuclear Weapon power.

2005-08 India and USA agreed to end 34 years of India's nuclear isolation, India get IAEA approved NSG waver, India-US Nuclear Pacts on 10 October 2008.

2014 Implementation Exercise begins.

The Nuclear world has recognised India's strength built over the past 70 years in the field of development of nuclear energy. The NSG endorsed Indo-US nuclear deal, may be designed to help India to meet its energy requirements without adding to the world's concerns for climate change. The agreements with USA, Russia, France and other nuclear power countries will enable India to enter into international trade for civilian use without any interference with our strategic nuclear programme, given the excellent quality of our nuclear scientists and technology. India would soon emerge as an important exporter of nuclear technology equipment for civilian purposes.

Presently, only three per cent of India's energy needs are met from the Nuclear sources. A growing India will have greater appetite for energy. We plan to produce 20,000 Megawatts of electricity generation from the nuclear sector by 2020, increasing it from the present 3700 Megawatts. India will enormously benefit from her access to the world's nuclear technology, equipment and materials as it would enable her to run its indigenous reactors at full capacity and generate more electricity which would mean more power for farmers, villages and industry. Nuclear energy will meet the twin challenges of energy security and environmental sustainability.

National Science and Technology and other Sectoral Policy Declarations of India (Select)

1948 Industrial Policy Resolution (revised in 1956)
1952 National Forest Policy
1958 The Scientific Policy Resolution
1968 National Education Policy
1970 The Patents Act
1972 The Wildlife (Protection) Act
1974 The Water (Preservation and Control of Pollution) Act
1977 The Water Cess Act

1978 Health for All (Population Policy)
1980 The Forest Conservation Act
1980 Industrial Policy Statement
1981 The Air (Preservation and Control of Pollution) Act
1983 Technology Policy Statement
1984 Ocean Policy Statement
1984 Computer Policy Statement
1986 National Education Policy
1986 Research and Development Cess Act
1986 Environment Protection Act
1986 Consumer Protection Act
1987 The Air (Prevention and Control of Pollution) Act, 1981 revised
1988 National Forest Policy revised of 1952
1988 The Water (Preservation and Control of Pollution, 1974) Act, revised
1991 National and Industrial Policy Statement
1992 National Policy on Education-1986 modified
1995 Technology Development Board Act
2000 National Textile Policy
2000 National Agricultural Policy
2002 Patents Act, modification of 1970
2002 The Biological Diversity Act
2002 The Wild Life (Protection) Amendment
2003 Science and Technology Policy
2006 Protection of the Environment
2007 National Urban Housing and Habitat Policy
2007 National Policy for Farmers
2008 Integrated Energy Policy
2008 Information Technology (Amendment) Act
2008 National Mineral Policy
2009 The Right to Education (RTE) Act
2010 Civil Liability for Nuclear Damage Act
2011 Nuclear Safety Regulatory Act
2011 National Manufacturing Policy
2013 Science, Technology and Innovation Policy
2013 National Food Security Act
2015 National Policy on Skill Development and Entrepreneurship
2015 Atomic Energy (Amendment) Act
2016 The Aadhaar (Targeted deliveries of financial and other subsidies benefits and services) Act
2016 National Intellectual Property Rights Policy
2017 National Health Policy

6
Defining Contributions

As India completes 70 years of its independence, it is time to introspect at the contribution of science and technology to national development. Several scientific and technological developments have touched the lives of common people in the last seven decades, though limelight is often hogged by achievements in fields like space and atomic energy.

In the past seven decades, India has built satellites and sent probes to the Moon and Mars, established nuclear power stations, acquired nuclear weapon capability and demonstrated firepower in the form of a range of missiles. Undoubtedly these are all fabulous achievements of Indian scientists and technologists.

At the same time, scientific research—combined with favourable public policies—has made India self-sufficient in production of food, milk, fruits and vegetables, drugs and vaccines. All this has had great social and economic impacts and directly and indirectly touched the lives of ordinary Indians. Developments in communications and information technology have enabled timely forecast of weather and early warning of cyclones, saving thousands of lives.

These are all results of investments made in scientific research soon after the independence and science-politics network built in decades prior to that. Investment in scientific research was 0.1 per cent of GNP in 1947. It went up to 0.5 per cent in less than a decade. Scientists like Shanti Swarup Bhatnagar, Homi Jehangir Bhabha and Prasanta Chandra Mahalanobis not only built scientific institutions but also helped shape policies.

Seven Defining Contributions

Here are seven defining contributions of Indian science and technology since 1947.

Green Revolution

In 1947, India produced about six million tonnes of wheat which was grossly inadequate to meet the total demand forcing the country to depend on large scale imports. With measures such as land reforms, improvements in irrigation facilities, fertilizer production and Intensive Agriculture District Programme, wheat production rose to 12 million in 1964—which was still insufficient to feed all Indians. While all this was going on, plant breeder Benjamin Peary Pal at the Indian Agriculture Research Institute was working on improving wheat varieties to achieve disease resistance and yield. The first breakthrough came in 1961 when a dwarf spring wheat variety with the Norin-10 dwarfing gene—developed by Normal Borlaug in Mexico—was grown in IARI. It had reduced height but long panicles. Later semi-dwarf varieties were grown in farmers' fields, yielding great results. These developments led to launch of the High Yielding Varieties Programme covering not just wheat but rice, maize, sorghum and pearl millet. The All India Coordinated Wheat Research Project under Pal remains an outstanding example of agriculture research. By 1970, wheat production went up to 20 million tonnes and rice production to 42 million tonnes. Thus, began the Green Revolution, making India self-sufficient in food grain production in the decades to come.

White Revolution

At the time of the independence, India was not only importing food grains but also milk products like baby food, butter and cheese. In 1955, India was importing 500 tonnes of butter and 3000 tonnes of baby food from dairy companies in Europe. The dairy movement had started in 1946 with the founding of the Kaira District Cooperative Milk Producers Union Limited under the leadership of Tribhuvandas Patel. In 1949, Verghese Kurien arrived in Anand to fulfil the condition laid down in the bond he had signed with the government at the time of going to America for higher education with government scholarship. He stayed back and became General Manager of the cooperative in 1950. The dairy faced a problem of fluctuating milk production as surplus milk would find no takers. European dairy companies were not willing to part with milk powder technology and were of the view that buffalo milk cannot be converted into milk powder. H.M. Dalaya, a young dairy engineer working with Kurien at Anand, demonstrated with experiments that buffalo milk can be converted into milk powder. Dalaya assembled a device using a spray paint gun and an air heater to make powder from buffalo milk, for the first time in the world. Later he showed that a commercially available machine, Niro Atomizer, could do the same. This laid the foundation for a dairy revolution in India and a national milk grid, making the country self-sufficient.

Satellite and Communication Revolution

When Vikram Sarabhai, as chairman of the Indian National Committee for Space Research, in mid-1960s envisioned the use of satellite technology for communication, remote sensing and weather prediction, few people believed him because India then did not possess any capability in building a rocket or a satellite. He wanted India to use space technology for education, health and rural development. Within a decade, India not only developed such a capability but demonstrated to the world peaceful use of space technology with the success of the Satellite Instructional Television Experiment (SITE), and the launch of Aryabhatta satellite from the Soviet Union. In another decade, Indian scientists launched the landmark INSAT and IRS series of satellites, bringing communication and television services to millions of people across the country. Timely prediction of weather events like cyclones using India-made satellites has helped save lives. Through pioneering use of the VSAT (Very Small Aperture Terminal) technology, banking and other services were revolutionised in the 1980s.

Drugs and Vaccines Manufacturing

India today is known as 'pharmacy of the world' as Indian companies are supplying affordable drugs and vaccines to not only developing but also to developed countries. It has been a long journey from the time when Indian drug industry was dominated by foreign companies whose drugs were prohibitively costly. In order to break the hold of multinational corporations, the central government established Hindustan Antibiotics Limited in 1954 and then the Indian Drugs and Pharmaceuticals Limited (IDPL) with Soviet assistance. These public sector units—along with national laboratories like National Chemicals Laboratory (NCL), Regional Research Laboratory, Hyderabad (now known as Indian Institute of Chemical Technology) and Central Drug Research Institute played a central role in generating necessary knowledge base and human resources needed for Indian industry to grow. The Patent Act of 1970 recognised only process patents, paving the way for Indian companies to make copies of patented drugs using alternative processes. CSIR labs developed processes for a range of drugs—ciprofloxacin, diclofenac, salbutamol, omeprazole, azithromycin etc.–and transferred the technology to private companies. Over next two decades, all this helped develop indigenous capabilities in both R&D and manufacturing.

C-DOT and Telecom Revolution

Like most other sectors, telecom sector too was dependent on supplies from multinational corporations, and due to high costs as well as shortage of foreign exchange new technology could not come in. The switching technology was considered strategic and only a handful of companies possessed it. The waiting period for a telephone line in India in the 1970s was several years, and connectivity in rural areas was extremely poor. The first attempt to develop an indigenous electronic exchange was initiated at the Telecom Research Centre (TRC) in the 1960s and the first breakthrough was a 100-line electronic switch developed in 1973. Around the same time, scientists at the Tata Institute of Fundamental Research

(TIFR), along with those from IIT, Bombay, developed a digital Automatic Electronic Switch for the army. These efforts got a boost in 1984 when the government established the Centre for Development of Telematics (C-DOT) by pooling scientific teams from TRC and TIFR under the leadership of Sam Pitroda. The rural telephone exchange developed by Indians could work under harsh conditions and without air conditioning. The technology developed in public sector was transferred for free to private companies, ending the monopoly of multinational giants and rapidly bringing connectivity to rural areas. C-DOT exchange became popular in dozens of developing nations.

IT Revolution and Railway Computerisation

The data processing industry in India during the decades after the independence was dominated by two multinationals—IBM and ICL. The data processing machines of these two firms were in use in the government, public sector, armed forces as well as research institutes. These companies brought old and discarded machines to India and leased them at high rentals. India needed latest computers for applications like National Sample Surveys, nuclear reactor development and other research. In order to break the monopoly of big companies and spur indigenous software and hardware development, the Department of Electronics was established in 1970. Public sector companies like Electronics Corporation of India Limited (ECIL), Computer Maintenance Corporation (CMC) and state electronics development corporations were established. The skills and knowledge thus developed got transferred to private industry. The first major application of information technology was the passenger reservation project of the Railways launched in 1986. It was the largest such project which demonstrated how technology can improve efficiency, cut corruption and touch the lives of millions without the need for them owning a digital gadget.

Blue Revolution

The 'blue revolution' refers to adoption of a set of measures to boost production of fish and other marine products. It was formally launched with the establishment of the Fish Farmers' Development Agency during the Fifth Five-year Plan in 1970. Later on, similar development agencies were set up for brackish water development to boost aqua-culture in several states. The objective of all this was to induce new techniques of fish breeding, rearing and marketing, as well as initiate production of other marine products like prawns, oysters, seaweeds, pearls and so on, using new techniques and scientific inputs. Scores of new technologies developed by research institutes under the Indian Council of Agriculture Research (ICAR) have been transferred to fish farmers all over the country.

7
Achievements

India ranks third among the most attractive investment destinations for technology transactions in the world. Dr. Harsh Vardhan, the present Union Minister of Department of Science and Technology, has reiterated that technology is a strong priority area for the government and it aims to make people science-centric. Modern India has had a strong focus on science and technology, realising that it is a key element of economic growth. India is among the topmost countries in the world in the field of scientific research, positioned as one of the top five nations in the field of space exploration. The country has regularly undertaken space missions, including missions to the moon and the famed Polar Satellite Launch Vehicle (PSLV).

Currently, twenty seven satellites including eleven that facilitate the communication network to the country are operational, establishing India's progress in the space technology domain. India is likely to take a leading role in launching satellites for the SAARC nations, generating revenue by offering its space facilities for use to other countries.

Market Size

India ranks second in terms of contribution to high-quality scientific research. It is among the world's top 10 nation in scientific publications. Position-wise, it is ranked 17th in the number of citations received and 34th in the number of citations per paper across the field of science and technology (among nations publishing 50,000 or more papers). The country is ranked ninth globally in the number of scientific publications and 12th in the number of patents filed.

India has been ranked as the top exporter of information and communication technology (ICT) services and second in innovation quality in 2017. The country has moved up six places to 60th position in the Global Innovation Index (GII).

Innovation centres are quickly being set up in India by organisations around the world, backed by the Government if India's move towards a digital economy and plenty of digital talent.

The Government of India is extensively promoting research parks technology business incubators (TBIs) and (RPs) which would promote the innovative ideas till they become commercial ventures.

India's Engineering R&D (ER&D) Globalisation and Services market reached US$ 22.3 billion in 2016 and is set to rise to US$ 38 billion by 2020. India has a total of 25 innovation centres in the country and has been ranked as the top innovation destination in Asia and second in the world for new innovation centres, according to a Capgemini report. The country accounts for 27 per cent of Asia's new innovation centres.

India's analytics is expected to touch US$ 16 billion by 2025 from the current US$ 2 billion, as per the National Association of Software and Services Companies (NASSCOM).

Developments/Investments

With support from the government, considerable investment and development has incurred in different sectors such as agriculture, healthcare, space research, and nuclear power through scientific research. For instance, India is gradually becoming self-reliant in nuclear technology. Recently, the Kudankulam Nuclear Power Project Unit-1 (KKNPP 1) with 1,000 MW capacity was commissioned, while the Kudankulam Nuclear Power Project Unit-2 (KKNPP 2) with 1,000 MW capacity is under commissioning.

Recent Developments

Some of the recent developments in the field of science and technology in India are as follows:

- As per the Government records, the number of Indian scientists coming back to India to pursue research opportunities has increased from 243 in 2007-12 to 649 between 2012 and 2017. In the span of five years 649 Indian scientists have returned to pursue research opportunities.
- India's space business to witness tremendous growth in the next five years, on the back of technology advancement, global space business opportunity and a sharp rise in Indian Space Research Organisation's (ISRO) satellite launch capability.

Investment Scenario

- Higher Education Funding Agency (HEFA) has approved projects US$ 320.89 million, of six institutions, which will be used to improve the research infrastructure in these institutions.
- Spending on artificial intelligence (AI) by Indian companies is

expected to increase by 8-11 per cent over the coming 18 months backed by rising influence of Al-based solutions across verticals.

- Grid Raster Inc, working in the virtual and augmented reality space, has raised US$ 2 million as seed funding, which will be used for marketing and product development.
- The State of Karnataka aims to become the electric vehicle (EV) capital of India with investments worth Rs. 31,000 crore (US$ 4.76 billion) from companies focusing on research and development (R&D) and manufacturing of EVs in the state.
- India has successfully launched the GSAT-17 satellite, which carries communication payloads in C-band, Extended C-band and S-band to provide various services to the country.

Government Initiatives

- A five year technology fund with US$ 4 million yearly investment, called Israel India Innovation Initiative Fund (I4F), has been launched by India and Israel to boost bilateral ties.
- Mr. Nitin Gadkari, the present Minister for Road Transport, Highways and Shipping, Government of India, is planning to introduce biofuel vehicles for road and water transportation on a large scale and has already directed NITI Aayog to conduct a research on methanol-powered vessels like cars and ships developed by China.
- The Department of Science and Technology (DST), Government of India has launched a scheme named 'Visiting Advanced Joint Research Faculty' (VAJRA), in a bid to bring together the Indian scientists abroad and India-based researchers for conducting joint researches in India.
- The Government of India aims to develop India into a global innovation hub by 2020 on the back of effective government measures taken to provide an enabling environment for growing research and development in India, says Mr. Y.S. Chowdary, the present Minister of State for Science and Technology Earth Sciences, Government of India.

Union Budget 2018-19

- The allocation to the Department of Science and Technology (DST) has been increased by 8.21 per cent to Rs. 5,114.78 crore (US$ 790.05 million) as against the previous budget.
- The budget for the Ministry of Science and Technology, has been increased by 6.11 per cent to Rs. 12,322.28 crore (US$ 1.9 billion) as against the previous budget.

- The Department of Atomic Energy has been allocated Rs. 13,971.41 crore (US$ 2.16 billion), an increase of 5.76 per cent against the previous budget.
- The Ministry of Earth Sciences was allocated Rs. 1,800 crore (US$ 278.04 million), which is an increase of 12.66 per cent as against the previous budget.

Road Ahead

India is aggressively working towards establishing itself as a leader in industrialisation and technological development. Significant developments in the nuclear energy sector are likely as India looks to expand its nuclear capacity. Moreover, nanotechnology is expected to transform the Indian pharmaceutical industry. The agriculture sector is also likely to undergo a major revamp, with the government investing heavily for the technology-driven Green Revolution. Government of India, through the Science, Technology and Innovation (STI) Policy-2013, among other things, aspires to position India among the world's top five scientific powers. 'Chandrayaan-2', India's space mission to moon, is set to take place between January-March 2018, stated Dr. Jitendra Singh, the present Union Minister of State (Independent Charge), Ministry of Development of North Eastern Region (DoNER), MoS PMO, Personnel, Public Grievances and Pensions, Atomic Energy and Space, Government of India.

8

Advancement and Enrichment

Over a period of time, India has progressively and perceptibly paved way for development in the field of science and technology.

The 21st century in India is apparently marked as the beginning towards an advancement in terms of technology and enrichment of knowledge base in the fields of Science.

At present, India holds a strong position in terms of advanced technology. India also serves as a knowledge warehouse with the existence of its many institutions catering to Science and Technology which come with qualified and trained manpower.

The different areas which undergo development with the advancement in Science and Technology are:

- Higher education
- Scientific research and development
- Technological development
- Advancement of agricultural system
- Development of space science and technology
- Development of medical science and technology
- Development of infrastructure
- Information and communication technology
- Development of various fields of engineering (including software, chemical, mechanical, civil, electrical, electronic, etc.)

Likewise, India has strong scientific and technological base that spreads across the country in the form of academic institutions, research and development laboratories, advanced medical centres (with research facilities), experimental centres, and different advanced industries.

Because of the development in all spheres of science and technology, today, India is unquestionably a leading developing country in the world.

Over the recent past, science and technology has made tremendous contribution towards the settlement of industries in India.

Starting from the micro level to the macro level, research and development in the field of technology has created an ideal niche for the overall growth of the economic condition of the country. The perceptible examples are the development of Atomic Energy, Space Science, dozens of successful satellite systems, advanced medical technologies, etc.

After the independence, it was not possible for India to depend on other countries for various aspects of development; therefore, the development of indigenous technology was indispensable for the overall development of a country.

Today, Indian technologies and companies are as competent as in other developed countries. India is also a lead in various fields, and is a tough competitor for other countries.

About the skilled human resources, many Indians are at top-notch positions in leading companies.

Indian industries started flourishing post 1990, i.e., the landmark era of globalisation, liberalisation, and privatisation, facilitated this growth. The industries catering to Information and Technology, Atomic Energy, Automotive, Biotechnology, Nanotechnology, Pharmaceutical, Petroleum, etc. have increased at global level.

On the other hand, the Government of India has also made sizable investment in the field of research and development to encourage the advancement of Indian economy, as stated earlier in second chapter.

How the security of a society directly related to the development of the technology is also discussed in chapter second.

Therefore, science and technology is like a boon for the overall scientific and economic development of the country.

9

Research and Development

Research and Development Expenditures

Investments in Indian science, measured in terms of Gross Expenditure on R&D (GERD), have shown a consistently increasing trend over the years. GERD has tripled in the last decade in nominal terms—from Rs. 24,117 crore in 2004-05 to Rs. 85,326 crore in 2014-15 and an estimated Rs. 1,04,864 crore in 2016-17–and double in real terms. However, as a fraction of GDP, public expenditures on research have been stagnant—between 0.6-0.7 percent of GDP—over the past two decades. Public expenditure is dominant, although its share has come down from three-fourths of all expenditures to about three-fifths.

About three-fifths of the public investment is spread over the key government science funding agencies like Atomic Energy, Space, Earth Sciences, Science and Technology and Biotechnology. Given the country 'severe health challenges, the low–and virtually stagnant in real terms'—budget of the ICMR is striking.

India's spending on R&D (about 0.6% of GDP) is well below that in major nations such as the US (2.8), China (2.1), Israel (4.3) and Korea (4.2). It is also unique in how dominant government is in carrying out R&D. In most countries, the private sector carries out the bulk of research and development even if government plays an important funding role. However, in India, the government is not just the primary source of R&D funding but also it is the primary user of these funds. Even more, government expenditure on R&D is undertaken almost entirely by the central government. There is a need for greater State Government spending, especially application oriented R&D aimed at problems specific to their economies and populations.

Private investments in research have severely lagged public investments in India. According to one analysis (Forbes, 2017) there are 26 Indian companies in the list of the top 2,500 global R&D spenders compared to 301 Chinese companies. Nineteen (of these 26) firms are in just three sectors: pharmaceuticals, automobiles and software. India has no firms in five of the top ten R&D sectors as opposed to China that has a presence in each of them.

India is also distinctive in another dimension: its universities play a relatively small role in the research activities of the country. Universities in many countries play a critical role in both creating the talent pool for research as well generating high quality research output. However, publicly funded research in India concentrates in specialised research institutes under different government departments. This leaves universities to largely play a teaching role—a decision that goes back to the 1950s. It is now widely acknowledged that whatever the merits of the decision at the time, this disconnection has severely impaired both teaching as well as the research enterprise in the country.

East Asian countries like China, Japan, and Korea, have seen dramatic increase in R&D as a percentage of GDP as they have become richer. India, on the other hand, has only seen a slight increase. In fact, in 2015, there was a sizeable decline in R&D spending even as GDP per capita continued to rise. At its current rate, India would just barely reach GERD of one per cent of GDP by the time it was as rich as the USA.

Ph.Ds in Science, Technology, Engineering, and Mathematics (STEM)

The other critical input for R&D is a well-trained workforce among which Ph.D students play an important role. Indian Ph.D students obtain their degrees either within India or abroad, especially in the US. There are less than half as many Ph.D students in STEM from India in the US as from China. It appears that fewer Indian students have been enrolling in recent years for such degrees, whether due to more attractive options after a master's degree or rising work visa challenges.

On the other hand, there has been an increase in Ph.D enrollments in India. In 2015-16 126,451 students were enrolled in Ph.D programmes in India, of which 62 per cent were in STEM fields (AISHE 2015-16). This increase is in part the result of concerted efforts by the government, including a substantial increase in the number and quantum of fellowships (such as the Prime Minister Research Fellowships at the IITs). Overall, though, India has far fewer researchers than other countries

Looking at publications and patents in India can help assess the productivity and quality of Indian research. In 2013, India ranked 6th in the world in scientific publications. Its ranking has been increasing as well. During 2009-14, annual publication growth was almost 14 per cent. This increased India's share in global publications from 3.1 percent in 2009 to 4.4 percent in 2014 as per the Scopus Database.

Broadly, the publication trends reveal that India is gradually improving its performance as measured by an important metric–publications. However, there is a downside to the increase in publications. There are many journals that publish non-peer-reviewed manuscripts for a substantial fee. The major catalyst for their explosive growth is "the demand created by increasing emphasis on the number of research publications as an important determinant of the academic performance of a faculty/scientist being considered for appointment or promotion

But in addition to increasing publications, trends in quality are also slowly improving. The *Nature Index* (which publishes tables based on counts of high-quality research outputs in the previous calendar year covering the natural sciences)—ranked India at 13 in 2017. But there is still a considerable lag in levels between India and the other two large countries, and the rate of improvement in China between 2001 and 2011 is dramatically better than India.

Patents

If journal publications reflect a country's prowess in science, patents reflect its standing in technology. According to the WIPO, India is the seven largest Patent Filing Office in the World. In 2015, India registered 45,658 patents in comparison to China (1,101,864), USA (589,410), Japan (318,721), Republic of Korea (213,694), and Germany (91,726). However, India produces fewer patents per capita.

Even in development time, the story is mixed. On one hand, much of India's low patent output could be due to its lower middle-income status. However, patents have grown much faster with income in countries like China, Korea, and Japan. Unless there is a greater focus on R&D, rising income alone will not allow India to catch up in the near future.

One major challenge in India has been the domestic patent system. While India's patent applications and grants have grown rapidly in foreign jurisdictions, the same is not true at home. Residential applications have increased substantially since India joined the international patent regime in 2005. However, the number of patents granted fell sharply post 2008 and has remained low. While Indian residents were granted over 5000 patents in foreign offices in 2015, the number for resident filings in India was little over 800.

The decrease in grants could have been due to a stricter examination process. But evidence suggests that there is a severe backlog and high rate of pendency for domestic patent applications. Reports indicate that due to manpower shortages there is a backlog of almost two lakh patents pending examination. In 2016-17, there were only 132 examiners for all patent applications in India. This has meant that patent examination and granting can take five or more years. Given the rapid rate of technological obsolescence, the inordinate delays in processing patents penalises innovation and innovators within the country.

The government's recent hiring of over 450 additional patent examiners and creation of an expedited filing system for Indian residents in 2017 will therefore be a welcome and crucial intervention to help fix the existing patent system. This chapter discusses the problems that pendency in patent litigation have had on innovation and business. Having addressed issues on the patent filing side, addressing patent litigation issues will also be crucial to ensuring that the patent system effectively rewards innovation.

Expanding R&D in India: The Way Forward

While the data discussed above presents a mixed view, many observers point to a more troubling picture. For example, a report submitted by a group of scientists has been quoted as saying: "The stature of Indian science is a shadow of what it used to be... because of decades of misguided interventions. We have lost self-confidence and ambition and the ability to recognize excellence amongst our own. In a false sense of egalitarianism, we often chose the mediocre at every level".

Clearly, India needs to redouble its efforts to improve science and R&D in the country first and foremost by doubling national expenditures on R&D with most of the increase coming from the private sector and universities. But the metrics also need to go beyond papers and patents to a broader contribution to providing value for society. What might these efforts entail? Some ideas are discussed below:

I. Improve math and cognitive skills at the school level

No country can create a vibrant super-structure of R&D with weak foundations of primary and secondary education for so many of its young. While India has made considerable strides in improving access to primary and secondary education, as discussed in Chapter 5, learning outcomes have been weak. This weakness denies India access to the intellect and energies of millions of young people.

II. Encourage investigator-led research

India needs to gradually move to have a greater share of an investigator-driven model for funding science research. A step in this direction occurred in 2008, with the establishment of the Science and Engineering Research Board (SERB), a statutory body of DST. This body has sanctioned about three and half thousand new R&D projects to individual scientists. It is a promising start that needs to expand with more resources and creative governance structures.

III. Increase funding for research from private sector as well as from state governments

The private sector should be incentivized to both undertake more R&D but to also support STEM research through CSR funds. Current tax law already favours CSR investment into R&D, but the types of R&D activities eligible can be expanded. Government can also work with the private sector to create new R&D funding opportunities which are also in line with private sector interests. Efforts like the 50 : 50 partnership with SERB for industry relevant research under the Ucchatar Avishkar Yojana (UAY) is a good example of what could help make such partnerships fruitful.

State governments too need to recognize the need to invest in application oriented research aimed at problems specific to their economies and populations. This would both strengthen state universities as well as provide much needed knowledge in areas such as crops, ecology and species specific to a state.

IV. Link national labs to universities and create new knowledge eco-systems

The separation of research from teaching has been an Achilles heel for Indian science.

Universities have students but need additional faculty support, while research institutes have qualified faculty but are starved of bright young students brimming with energy and ideas. A closer relationship between the two in specific geographic and spatial settings would help nurture research in areas reflecting the fields of science in which the national research centers have strengths. Together they can link up with the commercial sectors and help develop industrial clusters in those areas that draw on these research strengths and lay the foundations of innovation driven "smart cities."

If success in research requires a deep commitment to excellence, commercial success requires speed and nimbleness. Government rules such as those requiring L1 for procurement are simply not geared to providing the flexibility that is needed at the frontiers of research where speed, product quality and reliability make all the difference between success and failure.

V. Take a mission driven approach to R&D

India has the potential to be a global leader outright in a number of areas if it is willing to invest. However, this will require a deliberate focus in a few key areas. The potential missions given below were chosen for their strategic importance and potential for societal impact. This is an illustrative list which should be periodically revisited by the scientific community, government and other stakeholders.

VI. Leverage scientific diaspora

There are today more than 100,000 people with PhDs, who were born in India but are now living and working outside India (more than 91,000 in the U.S. alone). From 2003 to 2013, while the number of scientists and engineers residing in the US rose from 21.6 million to 29 million, the number of immigrant scientists and engineers went from 3.4 million to 5.2

million. Of this, the number from India increased from just above half million in 2003 to 950,000 in 2013.

However, with the strength of India's economy and growing anti-immigrant atmosphere in some Western countries, India has an opportunity to attract back more scientists. There has been an increase in the number of Indian scientists returning to work in India during the last five years, but the numbers are still modest (from 243 during 2007-12 to 649 in 2012-17) (Press Trust of India 2017).

There are a number of government programmes such as the Ramanujan Fellowship

Scheme, the Innovation in Science Pursuit for Inspired Research (INSPIRE) Faculty Scheme and the Ramalingaswami Re-entry Fellowship, that provide avenues to qualified Indian researchers residing in foreign countries, to work in Indian institutes/universities, and the Visiting Advanced Joint Research Faculty Scheme (VAJRA). These schemes could be enhanced to take advantage of opportunities to recruit in a way to build whole research groups; the inducements should be such as to allow them to do good research (laboratory resources, ability to hire post-docs, housing etc.) rather than financial, to ensure that home grown talent has a level playing field

VII. Improve the culture of research

Indian science and research institutes need to inculcate less hierarchical governance systems that are less beholden to science administrators and encourage risk-taking and curiosity in the pursuit of excellence. While the age of peak productivity of scientists has shifted upwards over the 20th century, it is still less than fifty. Great achievements in the sciences decline after middle age, and youth, conceptual achievement, and scientific revolutions are linked (Jones et. al. 2014). Hence it is imperative that there be greater representation of younger scientists in decision-making bodies in their areas of expertise.

VIII. Greater public engagement of the science and research establishment

If science is to garner greater support from society, it will require scientists to engage more vigorously with society. Much of science is—and should be—a public good, and hence that will always require substantial public funding. But the need for publicly funded science means that national laboratories and other publicly funded R&D institutions need to make much stronger efforts to engage with the public and not make their research centers quintessential ivory towers. This will require much greater efforts at science communication whether through the media or through regular tours and lectures for school and college students as well the general public. Scientists need to create broad public support for their work and not treat it as an entitlement, given the many claims on the public purse. And if they do that, they will find a receptive and supportive public.

10
Landscape

An overview of India's STI landscape with a particular focus on the policies and initiatives of the new government of PM Narendra Modi (in power since mid-2014) is discussed.

Methodology

- JNU-based STI policy expert (Prof. Venni V. Krishna, expert on Sociology of Research) was contracted to draft the report.
- Data collection through desk research and interviews (by Prof. Krishna and associates).
- Quality review through ZSI (ongoing).

Core Messages and Findings

- R&D investments in absolute terms increased almost fourfold.
- The private sector's share increased.
- Implemented institutional change affecting the research policy area:
  - The National Institution for Transforming India (NITI Aayog) replaced the earlier Planning Commission.
  - The National Innovation Council, established by the prior government in 2010/2011, is practically discontinued with the NITI Aayog and ministries taking over its functions.
- The current government continued the expansion of the top layer of federal higher education institutions also performing research. Since 2006, six Indian Institutes of Science Education and Research (IISERs) have been established. Their mandate is to perform frontier research in the basic sciences (as well as related higher education). The group of the more engineering and applied sciences oriented Indian Institutes of Technology (IITs) was also expanded.
- The largest number of R&D personnel, however, continues to be

employed in public research institutions (like the labs of the Council of Scientific and Industrial Research (CSIR) or of Ministries like the Department of Biotechnology, the Department of Atomic Energy, etc.).

- In terms of publication output, India's share in worldwide output rose from under to over 4 per cent in recent years.
- The prior government announced the 'Decade of Innovation' 2010-2020 and launched a Science, Technology and Innovation Policy in 2013 (STIP 2013).
- The new government endorsed the STIP 2013 policy. The visibility and prominence of STI topics increased with the new government. The current scenario is more decentralised.
- The new government announced a series of National Flagship Programmes/Schemes:
  - Make in India (promoting manufacturing in India; stirred by Ministry of Commerce and Industry);
  - Digital India (aiming to continue India's relative success in the ICT sector);
  - Skill India (a new Ministry of Skill Development and Entrepreneurship was launched);
  - Green India (focusing on renewable energy and innovation; electric vehicles);
  - Smart Cities and Urban Development (100 smart cities shall be built);
  - Clean India (Ganga Rejuvenation Programme with various ministries involved; plus the Clean India Campaign (Swachh Bharat Abhiyaan) focusing on clean neighbourhoods;
  - Creating New Infrastructure (ports, industrial corridors, etc.).
- Public R&D resources are expected in these programmes.
- The government has also announced a focus on the ease of doing business especially aiming at foreign investors (expanding the visa on arrival scheme, removing certain distinctions in FDI, etc.).
- Atal Innovation Mission (currently endowed with a budget of around € 20m) aims to provide an innovation promotion platform and related R&D funds. Its mandate states that it should promote a network of world-class innovation hubs (e.g. as part of IITs, IIMs, AIIMS, etc.).
- The new government also launched an FDI Policy 2015 and a new National IPR Policy.

11
Commitment

India's commitment to the use of science and technology as a key instrument in national development has been clearly articulated time and again in various policy documents right from the early years of independence.

And indeed, the progress made by our country since then in attainment of the stated goals in policy and plan documents has been substantial.

In the past decades 200 universities affiliating around 3000 colleges have been established to serve as an incubation ground for producing lakhs of technically qualified professionals.

India today is acknowledged as the third largest storehouse in the world for technically qualified workforce.

The pioneering Indian spirit has manifested itself in many fields; many frontiers have been won over.

Agricultural Research and Development

There was a time when Indian policy makers were worried about ways to feed the ever growing population. Limited forex reserves meant importing food was never a feasible idea, the other option was to bring more area under cultivation and that would have meant cutting the forests.

The solution was "Green Revolution" aimed at increasing the yield per hectare of land by using hybrid, high-yielding varieties of seeds.

Green Revolution

Under a man—a visionary whose dream was to rid the world of hunger and poverty, the great Dr. M.S. Swaminathan, better known as the "Father of the Green Revolution"—India developed into a country that fed itself.

Under the aegis of Indian Council of Agricultural Research, more than 2300 high yielding, hybrid varieties of food grains and cash crops have been developed. The achievements have been substantial by all means.

The Indian National Gene Bank established by the ICAR as a part of the National Bureau of Plant Genetic Resources, has preserved more than 1,50,000 accessions and samples. The capacity of this gene bank has been increased to about one million making it the largest gene bank of the world. It has more than 7100 accessions of underutilised crops.

World's first hybrid cotton, pearl millet, the first hybrid sorghum, the first hybrid castor, the first hybrid mango are some of the amazing achievements of Indian agricultural research.

After China, India is only the second country in the world to develop its very own hybrid rice.

The first amber coloured commercial Triticale dwarf and very high-yielding wheat varieties were developed by ICAR, thereby providing sustenance to millions of hungry Indians without actually cutting into the forest cover or being depended on imports.

Besides the green revolution, the yellow revolution in oil seeds, white revolution in milk production, blue revolution in fish production and golden revolution in horticulture bear ample testimony to the contribution of our agricultural scientists in making our country self sustained in terms of food production.

Bhakra Dam

The Bhakra Nangal dam in itself stands as a proud testimony to the technical prowess of Indian engineers. For all those NRIs who love to gawk at America's Hoover dam, it would come as a surprise that the Bhakra at 741 feet is one of the highest gravity dams (compare Hoover Dam at 732 ft). The dam provides irrigation to 10 million acres, thus playing a pivotal role in making the green revolution a true success.

Defence Research and Development

By far the most remarkable achievement of India in the S&T sphere is the triumph over innumerable international sanctions to develop indigenous defence infrastructure. The bigger the challenge, the more determined Indian scientist became.

Kaveri Engine

The GTX-35VS Kaveri is a low-bypass-ratio afterburning turbofan developed by the Gas Turbine Research Establishment (GTRE), a lab under DRDO. Kaveri engine is an indigenous Indian design intended to power production models of the HAL's Tejas fighter, also known as "Light Combat Aircraft" (LCA) as well as the proposed twin-engine Medium Combat Aircraft (MCA). Further evolution of the Kaveri design is envisioned for armoured fighting vehicles and for ship propulsion.

The Kaveri engine has been specifically designed for the demanding Indian operating environment, which ranges from hot desert to the highest mountain range in the world.

With its development India no longer has to go around the world begging for engines to power its indigenous fighter planes and launch vehicles.

Tejas

Tejas Light Combat Aircraft (LCA) is India's answer to the F-16s, understanding the pressing need to be self reliant in defence, it was developed indigenously by Hindustan Aeronautics Limited.

HAL's Tejas is an advanced, light weight, supersonic multi-role fighter aircraft. Its tailless compound delta wing design powered by a single engine makes it one of the best multi role aircrafts around.

Sonars

DRDO, Bharat Electronics Limited (BEL) and the Indian Navy have developed a range of Sonars for the Navy's frontline combat ships. These include the APSOH (Advanced Panoramic Sonar Hull mounted), HUMVAD (Hull Mounted Variable Depth sonar) and the HUMSA (Hull Mounted Sonar Array), Panchendriya Submarine sonar and fire control system, sonobuoy Tadpole, Simhika.

Sonars may be considered one of DRDO's most successful achievements, years of toil has now assured that today, the Indian Navy's most powerful ships rely on Indian made sonars.

Torpedoes

DRDO is currently developing multiple Torpedoes. These include a light weight torpedo (Advanced Experimental Torpedo). Apart from it DRDO is also developing heavy weight wire-guided torpedo Varunastra and Thakshak thermal torpedo suitable for use against both ships and submarines.

Prithvi

Prithvi Short Range Ballistic Missile: Three variants exist—the Prithvi I, II and III. Another submarine launched variant known as the K-15 is under development. The Prithvi is an exceptionally precise liquid fuelled missile with a range of up to 350 km. While relatively inexpensive and accurate, with a good payload, its logistics footprint is high, on account of it being liquid fuelled.

It is indeed one of the best ballistic missile in the world in its class.

Agni

Agni Missile series: The Agni-II is an Intermediate range ballistic missile with a range of up to 2500 kms. The Agni-I is a shorter ranged unit with a range of up to 800 kms. The Agni-III is meant for a longer ranged deterrence capability with a range of up to 6000 kms.

Akash

The Akash, a medium range SAM (surface to air missile) system comprising the command guided Akash missile and its specific launchers.

India's defence research programme is very symbolic in nature; it has showed to the world that even after being a late starter in the sphere of defence technology, India has developed on its own a credible defence arsenal.

As a result, India no longer has to go around the world begging for high-tech defence equipment to safe guard its frontiers.

Space Research

Since its advent, a significant feature of the Indian space programme has been the underlying emphasis on reaping its benefits in the shortest possible time. To achieve this objective simultaneous R&D was initiated in all the three spheres of space technology namely rocket, satellite and space infrastructure development.

Indian Satellite Systems

Indian Remote Sensing: The IRS system is by far the world's biggest constellation of remote sensing satellites. These satellites provide data for applications in agriculture, forestry, water harnessing, land use and land cover mapping, fold mapping and ocean resources survey.

INSAT: The Indian National Satellite (INSAT) system is a shining example of what all has been achieved by India's space technology. The INSAT series is the largest domestic communication system in the Asia-Pacific Region. Active satellites of this series include INSAT-2E, INSAT-3A, INSAT-3B, INSAT-3C, INSAT-3E, KALPANA-1 (METSAT), GSAT-2, EDUSAT (GSAT-3) and INSAT-4A. INSAT satellites provide transponders (about 150) in various bands (C, S, Extended C and Ku) to serve the television and communication needs of India.

The development of the INSAT system was a milestone by all means; it gave India the prowess to stand on its own for all critical functions.

INSAT and Development of India's Intellectual Capital

A land mark achievement of the INSAT series has been its role in helping unleash the power of distance learning. Never before had it happened that professors from India's premier educational institutes were accessible to students even in the remotest part of India. ISRO in association with UGC and Doordarshan through interactive shows like Gyan Vani brought about a silent revolution in the field of education.

Innumerable students from all parts of the country benefited from ISRO's novel methods, thereby immensely adding to India's intellectual capital.

Launch Vehicles: The Indian Satellite Launch Vehicle (SLV) was a project started in the early 1970s by ISRO to develop the technology needed to launch satellites. The project leader was Dr. A.P.J. Abdul Kalam. The first launch of the SLV took place in Sriharikota on 10 August 1979.

With its launch India joined the elite club of countries with such capabilities. Over the years the technological capabilities of India in this sphere have increased many folds; the SLV was followed by the ASLV (Augmented Satellite Launch Vehicle), the PSLV (Polar Satellite Launch Vehicle) and the latest of them all, the state-of-the-art GSLV (Geosynchronous Satellite Launch Vehicle).

The progress India has made in the field of space technology is incredible in all sense and can be best described in the words of present ISRO Chairman G. Madhavan Nair. The year was 1963; Madhavan Nair was in his final year at Thiruvananthapuram Engineering College, on the last day of his final year papers Madhavan Nair woke up early to make final preparations, to study alone he went to the hostel terrace.

Standing there he was witness to a very peculiar site, he saw a man cycling down the road towards Thumba with "something" resembling like a rocket on his cycle carrier. Closely following him, in fact, running behind the cycle was another young man. He was certainly intrigued but did not know he was about to witness history. The man cycling with the "rocket" was none other than the father of Indian space research Dr. Vikram Sarabhai and the man following him on foot was Dr. A.P.J. Abdul Kalam. They were on their way to Thumba to fire India's first sounding rocket Nicke Apache. After sometime Madhavan Nair witnessed a rocket rise on the western horizon. He had by chance become witness to ISRO's first space flight, an organisation he was destined to head one day.

Today India is one of the leading nations in the field of space technology. From launch vehicle technologies to satellite design, fabrication to its application in diverse areas like communication, broadcasting, meteorology, disaster management, telemedicine, etc. Indian scientists have successfully developed and demonstrated these all.

Not amongst those who rest on their past laurels, Indian space scientists have charted out ambitious plans to take Indian space programme to the next level.

India's first ever lunar orbital mission "Chandrayaan" is scheduled for mid-2008 lift-off. ISRO Chairman aims to put an Indian in space by 2015 and send an unmanned mission to Mars in the near future. And, with the successful testing of indigenously built Cryogenic engine, ISRO is confident of meeting its policy targets and take India one notch up on the global space arena.

Computing

PARAM

PARAM is the series of super-computers developed by the Centre for Development of Advanced Computing (C-DAC). The development of the same was taken up as a challenge to break the hegemony of the western world when it came to super-fast computing. The western world was reluctant to part with any of their technology as they feared India would use it for its space programme.

Indian scientists under Dr. Bhatkar developed something that was thought to be impossible until now. He functioned as the architect of PARAM Supercomputers, GIST multilingual technology and Education-To-Home (ETH) mission.

Technologies that had far reaching impact on India's emergence as a pioneer in super-fast computing.

The latest machine in the series is the PARAM Padma, which reached No. 171 on the TOP 500 in 2003. Others include PARAM 10000 and PARAM 9000/SS. The PARAM 10000 was India's first TFLOPS computer. C-DAC has also developed a high performance System Area Network called the PARAM Net-II having transfer speeds of up to 2.5 Gbit/s.

The major applications of PARAM 10000 are in weather forecasting, remote sensing, drug design and molecular modelling. PARAMs have also helped in India's space programme.

Future Challenges

Despite achieving a lot in the last 50 years, what is of paramount importance in the present context of fast changing technological scenario is to keep the momentum going and further the efforts in science and technological R&D.

The main challenge is to keep pace with the technological changes so as to ensure that the S&T developments are used for socio-economic development and help India develop into a country that can stand tall even amongst the tallest of the all.

12
Recent Developments

India ranks third among the most attractive investment destinations for technology transactions in the world. Dr. Harsh Vardhan, Union Minister of Department of Science and Technology, has reiterated that technology is a strong priority area for the government and it aims to make people science-centric. Modern India has had a strong focus on science and technology, realising that it is a key element of economic growth. India is among the topmost countries in the world in the field of scientific research, positioned as one of the top five nations in the field of space exploration. The country has regularly undertaken space missions, including missions to the moon and the famed Polar Satellite Launch Vehicle (PSLV).

India is likely to take a leading role in launching satellites for the SAARC nations, generating revenue by offering its space facilities for use to other countries.

India ranks 6th position for scientific publications and ranks at 10th for patents which included only resident applications. The number of patent applications filed by the Indian scientists and inventors increased to 47,857 in financial year 2018 from 46,904 in financial year 2016. India ranks 13th position at the Nature Index in 2017, based on counts of high-quality research outputs in natural sciences.

India improved its rank on the Global Innovation Index for the second year consecutively. From being ranked at the 81st position in 2015, India improved its ranking to 66th in 2016 and further to 60th in 2017.

The Government of India is extensively promoting research parks technology business incubators (TBIs) and (RPs) which would promote the innovative ideas till they become commercial ventures. India is world's third largest technology startup hub with incorporation of 1,000 new companies in 2017.

The engineering R&D and product development market in India is forecasted to grow at a CAGR of 20.55 per cent to reach US$ 45 billion by 2020 from US$ 28 billion in financial year 2018.

Developments/ Investments

With support from the government, considerable investment and development has incurred in different sectors such as agriculture, healthcare, space research, and nuclear power through scientific research. For instance, India is gradually becoming self-reliant in nuclear technology.

Recent Developments

Some of the recent developments in the field of science and technology in India are as follows:

- As per the Government records, the number of Indian scientists coming back to India to pursue research opportunities has increased from 243 in 2007-2012 to 649 between 2012 and 2017. In the span of five years 649 Indian scientists have returned to pursue research opportunities.
- India's space business to witness tremendous growth in the next five years, on the back of technology advancement, global space business opportunity and a sharp rise in Indian Space Research Organisation's (ISRO) satellite launch capability.

Investment Scenario

- Grid Raster Inc, working in the virtual and augmented reality space, has raised US$ 2 million as seed funding, which will be used for marketing and product development.
- India's R&D investments forecasted to increase to US$ 83.27 billion in 2018 from US$ 76.91 billion in 2017.

Government Initiatives

- In February 2018, Union Ministry of Science and Technology developed an interface to enable transfer of technologies from Council of Scientific and Industrial Research (CSIR) laboratories to small-scale industries.
- In February 2018, the Union Cabinet has approved implementation of 'Prime Minister Research Fellows (PMRF)' scheme, which will promote the mission of development through innovation, at a total cost of Rs 1,650 crore (US$ 245.94 million) for a period of seven years beginning 2018-19.
- In February 2018, Union Government of India announced grant of Rs 1,000 crore (US$ 155.55 million) for the second phase of Impacting Research Innovation and Technology (IMPRINT), a fund created by Department of Science and Technology and Ministry of Human Resource and Development.

- The Government of India granted Atal Innovation Mission with US$ 24.84 million will boost the academicians, entrepreneurs and researchers to work towards innovation.

Union Budget 2018-19

- The allocation to the Department of Science and Technology (DST) has been increased by 8.21 per cent to Rs 5,114.78 crore (US$ 790.05 million) as against the previous budget.
- The budget for the Ministry of Science and Technology, has been increased by 6.11 per cent to Rs 12,322.28 crore (US$ 1.9 billion) as against the previous budget.
- The Department of Atomic Energy has been allocated Rs 13,971.41 crore (US$ 2.16 billion), an increase of 5.76 per cent against the previous budget.
- The Ministry of Earth Sciences was allocated Rs 1,800 crore (US$ 278.04 million), which is an increase of 12.66 per cent as against the previous budget.

Road Ahead

India is aggressively working towards establishing itself as a leader in industrialisation and technological development. Significant developments in the nuclear energy sector are likely as India looks to expand its nuclear capacity. Moreover, nanotechnology is expected to transform the Indian pharmaceutical industry. The agriculture sector is also likely to undergo a major revamp, with the government investing heavily for the technology-driven Green Revolution. Government of India, through the Science, Technology and Innovation (STI) Policy-2013, among other things, aspires to position India among the world's top five scientific powers. Indian Space Research Organisation (ISRO) will launch its first Indian human mission by 2022.

13
Initiatives of NDA Government

Prime Minister Narendra Modi, while addressing the inaugural session of the 105th Indian Science Congress, exhorted scientists to extend their research from "labs" to "land" for the greater benefit of people and said time was ripe to refine R&D as research for development of nation. "Technology will allow greater penetration of services such as education, health care and banking to our citizens. Reaching the unreached through science and technology in most appropriate as science can solve the socio-economic problems of common people. Communicating scientific achievements to society will inculcate scientific temper among the people, particularly the youth," said Modi. He has been focusing on the importance of science and technology to national development, whenever he meets scientists and technologists.

Governments' Department of Science and Technology (DST) has been taxing several new initiatives to promoting innovation, supporting cutting edge research, attracting the youth towards science and technology, improving ease of doing science and fostering international collaboration.

Some of the S&T activities happened in recent times are the followings:

- Technology Day was celebrated on 11 May 2017 to commemorate India's success in taking science and technology to the service of the country. Technology Day commemorates India's success in using science and technology to address the challenges facing the country. On 11 May 1998, the Pokhran test was conducted. Atal Bihari Vajpayee, former Prime Minister, declared a full-fledged nuclear state after operation 'Shakti' and it made India the sixth country to join the Nuclear Club.
- India and UK Science and Technology Ministers received the progress made in India. UK partnerships in science, technology and innovations, which has been significantly intensified under the Newton-Bhaba programme.
- India and Canada Technology Summit was inaugurated on 14 November 2017 and opened a new chapter in their bilateral relationship. The summit was organised jointly by the Department

of Science and Technology of Government of India and Confederation of Indian Industry.

- Centenary celebrations of the Bose Institute in Kolkata were held in November 2017. This was one of the earliest scientific institutes established in India. It contributed much to research in the biological and physical sciences. It has very active social outreach programme in rural Bengal through its rural bio-technology initiative. It has been making an honest effort to spread the culture of science and innovation down to the grassroots of our society.
- Teacher Associates of Research Excellence (TARE) was formulated to activate the latent and unused R&D capacity in colleges and state universities that lack S&T infra structure and culture.
- Deen Dayal Upadhay Vigyan Gram Sankul Pariyojana was launched in 2017. It would formulate and implement appropriate S&T Interventions for Sustainable Development through cluster approach.
- India and Canada Technology Summit in November, 2017 opened a new chapter in their bilateral relationship.
- MANAK (Million Minds Augmenting National Aspiration and Knowledge) has been initiated to foster cultivate of scientific innovation among school children of Class VI to Class X.
- Some new initiatives initiated are:
  - Inter disciplinary Centre for Cyber Secretary and Cyber Security and Cyber Defence of Critical Infrastructures
  - Complete Online Processing of INSPIRE
  - ONLINE Web based System
  - India S&T Portal
  - Quantum Information Science and Technology
  - Materials on Energy Storage
- New Science and Technology Council formed to advise PM on science, technology and innovations. It includes noted mathematician from Princeton University, the first woman Dean of Armed Forces Medical College, Principal scientific advisor to the government of India, ISRO Chief, and other eminent scientists, besides secretaries of 10 Central Ministries.

The Committee will facilitate the formulation of policies and decisions, provide action-oriented and future preparedness advise and assist in directing S&T to solve the socio-economic problems in the country. It will also have a large focus on driving innovations in education, research, industry, etc.

Technology Vision Document 2035

- The Prime Minister unveiled the 'Technology Vision Document 2035' while inaugurating the 103rd Indian Science Congress on

3rd January 2016. The document foresees the Indians of 2035, and technologies required for fulfilling their needs. It is not a visualisation of technologies that will be available in 2035, but a vision of where our country and its citizens should be in 2035 and how technology should bring this vision to fruition.

- The document is dedicated to late Dr. A.P.J. Abdul Kalam, the former President of India.
- The Aim of this 'Technology Vision Document 2035' is to ensure the Security, Enhancing of Prosperity, and Enhancing Identity of every Indian, which is stated in the document as "Our Aspiration" or "Vision Statement" in all languages of the 8th Schedule of the Constitution.
- The Prime Minister has hoped that the 12 Sectoral Technology roadmaps being prepared by Technology Information, Forecasting and Assessment Council, (TIFAC), which is also the author of this 'Technology Vision 2035' document, would excite our scientists and decision makers. Roadmaps, when prepared, will be presented to the Government of India and they would lead for further adoption of technologies in those sectors.

  The 12 identified sectors of Vision Document are as follows:

  1. Education
  2. Medical Sciences and Healthcare
  3. Food and Agriculture
  4. Water
  5. Energy
  6. Environment
  7. Habitat
  8. Transportation
  9. Infrastructure
  10. Manufacturing
  11. Materials
  12. Information and Communication Technology
- The Vision documents also identifies twelve (12) prerogatives (six for meeting individual needs and six for the collective needs) that should be available to each and every Indian. These are as follows:

Individual Prerogatives

- Clean air and potable water
- Food and nutritional security
- Universal healthcare and public hygiene
- 24×7 energy
- Decent habitat
- Quality education, livelihood and creative opportunities

Collective Prerogatives

- Safe and speedy mobility
- Public safety and national security
- Cultural diversity and vibrancy
- Transparent and effective governance
- Disaster and climate resilience
- Eco-friendly conservation of natural resources

- The vision document also makes a mention of three critical essential pre-requisites or Transversal Technologies i.e., materials, manufacturing and Information and Communication Technology (ICT) to provide the foundation upon which all other technologies would be constructed.
- The document also talks of required infrastructure which it says primarily include relevant knowledge institutions besides ports, highways, airports, railways, cold chains, etc. Among the essential prerequisites, it also mentions fundamental research in the fields of physics, chemistry, biology and other allied sciences.
- There has also been a raging debate on the Social Impact of technology and the choice between capital intensive and manpower intensive. Capital intensive technology, especially in India with abundant human resources, has been projected as detrimental to the use of 'Manpower' as it is argued that it would reduce jobs. The Vision Document seeks to bust this myth by arguing in favour of judicious policy and conscious planning in employing technology to impart new skills to the manpower and fulfill needs of the society. It visualises technology as a great leveler rather than as an enhancer of social stratification.
- In order to overcome these challenges, the Vision Document 2035 envisages a rational assessment of the capabilities and constraints of the Indian Technological Landscape. It categorises technologies into a five-fold classification from an Indian perspective which is as follows:
  - (A) *Technology Leadership*—niche technologies in which we have core competencies, skilled manpower, infrastructure and a traditional knowledge base e.g., Nuclear Energy, Space Science.
  - (B) Technology Independence—strategic technologies that we would have to develop on our own as they may not be obtainable from elsewhere e.g., Defence sector.
  - (C) *Technology Innovation*—linking disparate technologies together or making a breakthrough in one technology and applying it to another e.g., solar cells patterned on chlorophyll based synthetic pathway are a potent future source of renewable energy.
  - (D) *Technology Adoption*—obtain technologies from elsewhere,

modify them according to local needs and reduce dependence on other sources e.g., foreign collaboration in the sectors of rainwater harvesting, agri-biotech, desalination, energy efficient buildings.

(E) *Technology Constraints*—areas where technology is threatening and problematic i.e. having a negative social or environmental impact because of serious legal and ethical issues e.g., Genetically Modified (GM) Crops.

- The Vision Document, in a separate section, gives a 'Call to Action' to all the key stakeholders. It brings to notice that for long term sustainability of India's technological prowess, it is important that:
  1. Technical Education Institutions engage in advanced research on a large scale leading to path-breaking innovations.
  2. Government enhances its financial support from the current one per cent to the long-envisaged two per cent of the GDP.
  3. The number of full-time equivalent Scientists in the core research sector should increase.
  4. Private Sector Participation and Investment in evolving technologies that is readily deployable and is translatable from lab to field thereby increasing efficiency in terms of technology and economic returns.
  5. Academia-Intelligentsia-Industry connect is established via idea exchange, innovative curricula design, based on the needs of the industry, industry-sponsored student internships and research fellowships inter alia.
  6. Creation of a Research Ecosystem so as to achieve the translation of research to technology product/process by integrating students, researchers and entrepreneurs.
- The document also identifies three key activities as a part of the 'Call to Action'. The first being knowledge creation. It says that India cannot afford not to be in the forefront of the knowledge revolution, either applied or pure. The second activity that cannot be reflected, it says is ecosystem design for innovation and development. The document again interestingly says that the primary responsibility for ecosystem design must necessarily rests with government authorities. A third key activity that it mentions is technology deployment with launching certain national missions involving specific targets, defined timelines requiring only a few carefully defined identified players.
- While this Vision document walks towards the future taking into consideration the country as a whole, the technology roadmap of each sector would provide of outlining future technology trends, R&D directives, pointers for research, anticipated challenges and policy imperatives pertaining to each sector.

14
Institutes of Technology

1. Indian Institutes of Technology

The Indian Institutes of Technology (IITs) are autonomous public institutes of higher education, located in India. They are governed by the *Institutes of Technology Act, 1961* which has declared them as "institutions of national importance" and lays down their powers, duties, and framework for governance, etc. The Institutes of Technology Act, 1961 lists twenty-three institutes (after the last amendment in 2016). Each IIT is an autonomous institution, linked to the others through a common IIT Council, which oversees their administration. The Minister of Human Resource Development is the ex-officio Chairperson of IIT Council. As of 2018, the total number of seats for undergraduate programmes in all 23 IITs is 11,279.

The first IIT was set up in Kharagpur in 1951, and soon later in Bombay (1958), Madras (1959), Kanpur (1959) and Delhi (1963). An IIT was then established in Guwahati in 1994. The University of Roorkee was converted to IIT Roorkee in 2001. Eight new IITs were set up in Gandhinagar, Jodhpur, Hyderabad, Indore, Patna, Bhubaneswar, Ropar, and Mandi in 2008-09. Around the same time the Institute of Technology, Banaras Hindu University was given IIT status. Another six new IITs in Tirupati, Palakkad, Dharwad, Bhilai, Goa and Jammu, were established in 2015-16, along with the conversion of ISM Dhanbad to IIT.

The IITs have a common admission process for undergraduate admissions, the Joint Entrance Examination—Advanced, formerly called the IIT-JEE until 2012. JEE Advanced admits students according to their ranks in the exam. The post-graduate level programme that awards M.Tech., MS degrees, and the doctoral programme that offers Ph.D in engineering is administered by the older IITs. M.Tech. and MS admissions are done on the basis of Graduate Aptitude Test in Engineering (GATE). Additionally, IITs also award other graduate degrees such as M.Sc. in Maths, Physics and Chemistry, MBA, etc. Admission to these programmes of IITs is done through Common Admission Test (CAT), Joint Admission Test for M.Sc. (JAM) and Common Entrance Examination for Design

(CEED). IIT Guwahati and IIT Bombay offer undergraduate design programmes as well. Joint Seat Allocation Authority conducts the joint admission process for a total of 23 IITs that offer admission for 10,962 seats.

Organizational Structure

The President of India is the most powerful person in the organisational structure of IITs, being the ex officio Visitor, and having residual powers. Directly under the President is the IIT Council, which comprises the minister-in-charge of technical education in the Union Government, the Chairmen of all IITs, the Directors of all IITs, the Chairman of the University Grants Commission, the Director General of CSIR, the Chairman of IISc, the Director of IISc, three members of Parliament, the Joint Council Secretary of Ministry of Human Resource and Development, and three appointees each of the Union Government, AICTE, and the Visitor.

Under the IIT Council is the Board of Governors of each IIT. Under the Board of Governors is the Director, who is the chief academic and executive officer of the IIT. Under the Director, in the organisational structure, comes the Deputy Director. Under the Director and the Deputy Director, come the Deans, Heads of Departments, Registrar, and President of the Students' Council.

Undergraduate Education

The Bachelor of Technology (B.Tech) degree is the most common undergraduate degree in the IITs in terms of student enrollment, although dual degrees integrating Master of Science or Master of Arts are also offered. The B.Tech course is based on a 4-year programme with eight semesters, while the Dual Degree and Integrated courses are 5-year programmes with ten semesters. In all IITs, the first year of B.Tech and Dual Degree courses are marked by a common course structure for all the students, though in some IITs, a single department introduction related course is also included. The common courses include the basics from most of the departments like Electronics, Mechanics, Chemistry, Electrical and Physics. At the end of first year (the end of first semester at IIT Madras, IIT Hyderabad and IIT Roorkee), an option to change departments is given to meritorious students on the basis of their performance in the first two semesters. Few such changes ultimately take place as the criteria for them are usually strict, limited to the most meritorious students.

From the second year onwards, the students study subjects exclusively from their respective departments. In addition to these, the students have to take compulsory advanced courses from other departments in order to broaden their education. Separate compulsory courses from humanities and social sciences department, and sometimes management courses are also enforced. In the last year of their studies, most of the students are placed into industries and organisations via the placement process of the respective IIT, though some students opt out of this either when going for higher studies or when they take up jobs by applying to the companies directly.

Master's Degrees and Postgraduate Diplomas

The IITs offer a number of postgraduate programmes including Master of Technology (B.Tech), Master of Business Administration (MBA) (only for engineers and post graduates in science), and Master of Science (MSc). Some IITs offer specialised graduate programmes such as Master of Design (M.Des.), the Post Graduate Diploma in Information Technology (PGDIT), Master in Medical Science and Technology (MMST), Master of City Planning (MCP), Master of Arts (MA), Postgraduate Diploma in Intellectual Property Law (PGDIPL), and the Postgraduate Diploma in Maritime Operation and Management (PGDMOM).

Some of the IITs offer an M.S. (by research) programme; the B.Tech and M.S. are similar to the US universities' non-thesis (course based) and thesis (research based) masters programmes respectively. Admissions to masters programmes in engineering are made using scores of the Graduate Aptitude Test in Engineering (GATE), while those to masters programmes in science are made using scores of the Joint Admission Test to M.Sc. (JAM).

Several IITs have schools of management offering master's degrees in management or business administration.

Bachelors-Masters Dual Degrees

The IITs also offer an unconventional B.Tech and B.Tech integrated educational programme called "Dual Degree". It integrates undergraduate and postgraduate studies in selected areas of specialisation. It is completed in five years as against six years in conventional B.Tech (four years) followed by an B.Tech (two years). Integrated Master of Science programmes are also offered at few IITs which integrates the Undergraduate and Postgraduate studies in Science streams in a single degree programme against the conventional University system. These programmes were started to allow IITians to complete postgraduate studies from IIT rather than having to go to another institute.

Doctoral Degrees

The IITs also offer the Doctor of Philosophy Degree (Ph.D) as part of their doctoral education programme. In it, the candidates are given a topic of academic interest by the professor or have to work on a consultancy project given by the industries. The duration of the programme is usually unspecified and depends on the specific discipline. Ph.D candidates have to submit a dissertation as well as provide an oral defence for their thesis. Teaching Assistantships (TA), and Research Assistantships (RA) are often provided.

The IITs, along with NITs and IISc, account for nearly 80 per cent of all engineering Ph.Ds in India. IITs now allow admission in Ph.D programmes without the mandatory GATE score

Academic Rankings

Nationwide, most IITs are ranked above any other engineering college in India in engineering rankings. *Outlook India*'s Top Engineering Colleges of 2017 ranked four IITs in its top 10, including the top four positions. Worldwide however, the highest ranked IIT (IIT Delhi) is ranked at 172 in the QS World University Rankings, followed by IIT Bombay ranked at 162, while other premier institutes as IISc Bangalore (ranked at 170) and three other IITs (IIT Madras at 264, IIT Kanpur at 293 and IIT Kharagpur at 308) make the top 310. In the 2017 QS World Rankings by Subject—IIT (ISM) Dhanbad featured at 24th followed by IIT Kharagpur at 35th position in the Engineering-Mining and Mineral science. IIT Delhi secures 49th place for Electrical Engineering in the same ranking. The only Institute that was listed in the top 400 by Times Higher Education rankings 2018 was IIT Bombay in the 351-400 category. The Times Asia Rankings 2018 featured IIT Bombay, IIT Kharagpur, IIT Roorkee, IIT Kanpur and IIT Delhi at 44th, 60th, 65th, 81st and 86th respectively. In 2016, a new IIT, IIT Indore was ranked 8th in the world followed by IIT Kanpur (which was ranked 9th) under a ranking released by Hackerrank for the world's best coders. The following IITs have topped the 2018 QS BRICS rankings: IIT Bombay (9), Delhi (17), Madras (18), Kanpur (21), Kharagpur (24), Roorkee (51), Guwahati (52), Hyderabad (100), Patna (108).

Criticism

The IITs have faced criticism from within and outside academia. Major concerns include allegations that they encourage brain drain and that their stringent entrance examinations encourage coaching colleges and skew the socio-economic profile of the student body. Recently some prominent IITians have also questioned the quality of teaching and research in IITs.

Brain Drain

Among the criticisms of the IIT system by the media and academia, a common notion is that it encourages brain drain. This trend has been reversed somewhat (dubbed the reverse brain drain) as hundreds of IIT graduates, who have pursued further studies in the USA, started returning to India in the 1990s. Additionally, IIT alumni are giving back generously to their parent institutions (examples are Kanwal Rekhi to IIT Bombay, Dr. Prabhakant Sinha to IIT Kharagpur, and many others). Until liberalisation started in the early 1990s, India experienced large scale emigration of IITians to developed countries, especially to the United States. Since 1953, nearly twenty-five thousand IITians have settled in the USA. Since the

USA benefited from subsidised education in IITs at the cost of Indian taxpayers' money, critics say that subsidising education in IITs is useless. Others support the emigration of graduates, arguing that the capital sent home by the IITians has been a major source of the expansion of foreign exchange reserves for India, which, until the 1990s, had a substantial trade deficit.

The extent of intellectual loss receded substantially over the 1990s and 2000s, with the percentage of students going abroad dropping from as high as 70 per cent at one time to around 30 per cent in 2005. This is largely attributed to the liberalisation of the Indian economy and the opening of previously closed markets. Government initiatives are encouraging IIT students into entrepreneurship programmes and are increasing foreign investment. Emerging scientific and manufacturing industries and outsourcing of technical jobs from North America and Western Europe have created opportunities for aspiring graduates in India. Many undergraduates go abroad to pursue further studies, such as MS, MBA and Ph.D.

2. National Institutes of Technology

The National Institutes of Technology (NITs) are autonomous public institutes of higher education, located in India. They are governed by the National Institutes of Technology Act, 2007, which declared them as "institutions of national importance" alongside Indian Institutes of Technology. These institutes of national importance receive special recognition from the Government of India. The NIT Council is the supreme governing body of India's National Institutes of Technology (NIT) system and all 31 NITs are funded by the Government of India. These institutes are among the top ranked engineering colleges in India and have one of the lowest acceptance rates for engineering institutes, of around 2 to 3 percent, second only to the Indian Institutes of Technology (IITs) in India. All NITs are autonomous which enables them to set up their own curriculum. The language of instruction is English at all these institutes.

NITs offer degree courses at bachelors, masters, and doctorate levels in various branches of engineering, architecture, management and science. Admission to the under-graduate courses such as Bachelor of Technology (B.Tech.) and Bachelor of Architecture (B.Arch) programmes in NITs are through the highly competitive Joint Entrance Examination (Main). Admission to postgraduate courses are through the Graduate Aptitude Test in Engineering for Master of Technology (M.Tech.) and Master of Science (M.Sc.) programmes, Common Admission Test for Master of Business Administration (MBA) programme and NIMCET for Master of Computer Applications (MCA) programme.

Since 2015, the Joint Seat Allocation Authority and Centralised

Counselling for M.Tech/M.Arch and M.Plan conduct the admission process for undergraduate and postgraduate programmes respectively in all NITs. As of 2017, the total number of seats for undergraduate programmes is 19,000 and for post graduate programmes is 8,050 in all 31 NIT.

During the second five-year plan (1956–60) in India, a number of industrial projects were contemplated. To ensure enough supply of trained personnel to meet the demand for these projects, a decision was taken to start the Regional Engineering Colleges (RECs), at the rate of one per each major state, which can churn out graduates with good engineering merit.

These were large-sized institutions judged by the standards then prevailing in the country. The considerations that weighed in this decision were:

A large-sized college would be more efficient than the equivalent small colleges, the proposed colleges have to meet the additional requirements of the country as a whole and for that purpose should have to function on an all-India basis. Therefore, the smaller they are in number and the larger in size, the better, and for the same reason their location is important from an all-India point of view.

The RECs were jointly operated by the central government and the concerned state government. Non-recurring expenditures and expenditures for post-graduate courses during the REC period were borne by the central government while recurring expenditure on undergraduate courses was shared equally by central and state governments.

The success of technology-based industry led to high demand for technical and scientific education. Due to the enormous costs and infrastructure involved in creating globally respected Indian Institutes of Technology (IITs), in 2002 Ministry of Human Resource Development (MHRD) Minister Murli Manohar Joshi decided to upgrade RECs to "National Institutes of Technology" (NITs) instead of creating IITs. The central government controls NITs and provides all funding. In 2002, all RECs became NITs.

The upgrade was designed along the lines of the Indian Institutes of Technology (IITs) after it was concluded that RECs had potential as proven by the success of their alumni and their contributions in the field of technical education. Subsequently, funding and autonomy for NITs increased, and they award degrees which have raised their graduates' perceived value. These changes implemented recommendations of the "High Powered Review Committee" (HPRC). The HPRC, chaired by R.A. Mashelkar, submitted its report entitled "*Strategic Road Map for Academic Excellence of Future RECs*" in 1998.

In 2004, MHRD issued NIT status to three more colleges, located at Patna (Bihar Engineering College, a 110-year-old college), Raipur (Government Engineering College), and Agartala (Tripura Engineering

College). Based on the request of state governments and feasibility, future NITs are either converted from existing institutes or can be freshly created. The 21st (and the first brand-new) NIT is planned for Imphal in the north-eastern state of Manipur at an initial cost of Rs. 500 crore. In 2010, the government announced setting up ten new NITs in the remaining states/ territories. This would lead to every state in India having its own NIT.

With the technology based industry's continuing growth, the government decided to upgrade twenty National Institutes of Technology to full-fledged technical universities. Parliament passed enabling legislation, the National Institutes of Technology Act in 2007 and took effect on 15 August of that year. The target is to fulfill the need for quality manpower in the field of engineering, science, and technology and to provide consistent governance, fee structure, and rules across the NITs. The law designates each NIT an Institute of National Importance (INI).

Organisational Structure

The President of India is the ex officio visitor of all the NITs. The NIT Council works directly under him and it includes the minister-in-charge of technical education in Central Government, the Chairmen and the Directors of all the NITs, the Chairman of University Grants Commission (UGC), the Director General of Council of Scientific and Industrial Research (CSIR), the Directors of other selected central institutions of repute, members of Parliament, Joint Council Secretary of Ministry of Human Resource Development (MHRD), nominees of the Central Government, All India Council for Technical Education (AICTE), and the Visitor.

- Two respective representing large, medium and small scale industries to be nominated by Central Government.
- One Professor and one Assistant Professor of the institute by rotation.

The Director serves under the Board of Governors, and is the school's chief academic and executive officer. Academic policies are decided by its Senate, which is composed of some professors and other representatives. The Senate controls and approves the curriculum, courses, examinations, and results. Senate committees examine specific academic matters. The teaching, training, and research activities of various departments of the institute are periodically reviewed to maintain educational standards. The Director is the ex officio Chairman of the Senate. The Deputy Director is subordinate to the Director. Together they manage the Deans, Heads of Departments, Registrar, President of the Students' Council, and Chairman of the Hall Management Committee. Deans and Heads of Departments in NITs are administrative postings rather than career paths. Faculty members serve as Deans and Heads of Departments for limited periods, typically 2 to 3 years, then returning to regular faculty duties. The Registrar is the chief administrative officer and overviews day-to-day operations. Below the Head of Department (HOD), are the various faculty members (professors, assistant professors, and lecturers). The Warden serves under the Chairman of the Hall Management Committee.

National Institutes of Technology Act

The National Institutes of Technology, Science Education and Research Act, 2007 was enacted by the Parliament of India to declare India's National Institutes of Technology as Institutes of National Importance. The Act received the assent of the President of India on 5 June 2007 and became effective on Independence Day, 2007. The National Institutes of Technology Act is the second law for technical education institutions after the Indian Institutes of Technology Act of 1961.

NIT Council

The NIT Council is the supreme governing body of India's National Institutes of Technology (NIT) system. The NIT Council consists of chairmen, directors of all NITs along with the government nominees from various sectors with the Minister of Human Resource Development as the Chairman of the Council. The NIT Council is the highest decision making body in the NIT fraternity and is answerable only to the Government of India. The NIT Council is expected to meet regularly and take steps conducive for maximum growth of the NITs as a whole in the near future.

Education

The NITs along with the IITs receive comparatively higher grants than other engineering colleges in India. Average NIT funding increased to 100 crore ($15.4 million) by year 2011. On average, each NIT also receives 20-25 crore ($3-3.8 million) under World Bank funded Technical Education Quality Improvement Programme (TEQIP I and TEQIP II). Other sources of funds include student fees and research funding from industry and contributions from the alumni. The faculty-to-student ratio in the NITs is between 1:7 and 1:9. The cost borne by undergraduate students is around Rs. 125,000 ($1934) per annum. After students from SC and ST categories, physically challenged students will now be the beneficiaries of fee waiver at the NITs in India

The various NITs function autonomously, and their special status as Institutes of National Importance facilitates the smooth running of NITs, virtually free from both regional as well as student politics. Such autonomy means that NITs can create their own curricula and adapt rapidly to the changes in educational requirements, free from bureaucratic hurdles. The medium of instruction in all NITs is English. The classes are usually held between 8:30 am and 5:30 pm, though there are some variations within each NIT. All the NITs have public libraries for the use of their students. In addition to a collection of prescribed books, the libraries have sections for fiction and other literary genres. Electronic libraries allow students access to online journals and other periodicals through the AICTE-INDEST consortium, an initiative by the Ministry of Human Resource Development. Students also have access to IEEE documents and journals.

Undergraduate Education

The Bachelor of Technology (B.Tech) degree is the most common undergraduate degree in the NITs in terms of student enrollment. The B.Tech course is based on a 4-year programme with eight semesters, while the Dual Degree and Integrated courses are 5-year programmes with ten semesters. In all NITs, the first year of B.Tech and Dual Degree courses are marked by a common course structure for all the students, though in some NITs, a single department introduction related course is also included. The common courses include the basics from most of the departments like Electronics, Mechanics, Chemistry, Electrical and Physics. At the end of first year, some NITs offer an option to the meritorious students to change departments on the basis of their performance in the first two semesters. Few such changes ultimately take place as the criteria for them are usually strict, limited to the most meritorious students. Few NITs also offer 5-year Bachelor of Architecture (B.Arch.) and 4-year Bachelor of Science (B.Sc.) degrees.

From the second year onwards, the students study subjects exclusively from their respective departments. In addition to these, the students have to take compulsory advanced courses from other departments in order to broaden their education. Separate compulsory courses from humanities and social sciences department, and sometimes management courses are also enforced. In the last year of their studies, most of the students are placed into industries and organisations via the placement process of the respective NIT, though some students opt out of this either when going for higher studies or when they take up jobs by applying to the companies directly.

Postgraduate and Doctoral Education Master Degrees

The NITs offer a number of postgraduate programmes including Master of Technology (B.Tech), Master of Business Administration (MBA), Master of Science (M.Sc.) and Master of Computer Applications (MCA). Some of the NITs offer an M.S. (by research) programme; the B.Tech and M.S. are similar to the US universities' non-thesis (course based) and thesis (research based) masters programmes respectively. Admissions to Masters programmes in engineering are made using scores of the Graduate Aptitude Test in Engineering (GATE), while those to masters programmes in science are made using scores of the Joint Admission Test to M.Sc. (JAM).

Three NITs, NIT Allahabad, NIT Trichy and NIT Rourkela have schools of management offering master's degrees in management or business administration.

Bachelors-Masters Dual Degrees

The NITs also offer an unconventional B.Tech and B.Tech integrated educational programme called "Dual Degree". It integrates undergraduate and postgraduate studies in selected areas of specialisation. It is completed in five years as against six years in conventional B.Tech (four years) followed by an B.Tech (two years). Integrated Master of Science programmes are also offered at few NITs which integrates the Undergraduate and Postgraduate studies in Science streams in a single degree programme against the conventional University system. These programmes were started to allow NITians to complete postgraduate studies from NIT rather than having to go to another institute. NIT Rourkela has such system.

Doctoral Degrees

The NITs also offer the Doctor of Philosophy Degree (Ph.D) as part of their doctoral education programme. In it, the candidates are given a topic of academic interest by the professor or have to work on a consultancy project given by the industries. The duration of the programme is usually unspecified and depends on the specific discipline. Ph.D candidates have to submit a dissertation as well as provide an oral defence for their thesis. Teaching Assistantships (TA), and Research Assistantships (RA) are often provided. The NITs, along with IITs and IISc, account for nearly 80 per cent of all engineering Ph.Ds in India.

15

Institutes of Science

Indian Institute of Science (IISc) is a public institute for research and higher education in science, engineering, design, and management. It is located in Bangalore, India, was established in 1909 with active support from Jamshedji Tata and H.H. Sir Krishnaraja Wodeyar IV, the Maharaja of Mysore. It is also locally known as the "Tata Institute". It was granted the Deemed University status in 1958.

Academic Programmes

Doctoral Degree Programmes

Research students constitute more than 70 per cent of the students on the campus. Ph.D. degrees offered in 40 different disciplines. Research programmes leading to doctoral degrees are the main thrust in many departments. The programme has a limited amount of course work, essentially to prepare the student to carry out the research, but the main emphasis is on the thesis work. The annual intake of research students is approximately 250 with several candidates sponsored from educational institutions and industries. The research students constitute the largest group (50%) on the campus.

The Integrated Ph.D programme is designed to offer opportunities to 3-year B.Sc. graduates for pursuing advanced research in areas of biological, chemical, mathematical, and physical Sciences, leading to the Ph.D degree.

Masters Degree Programmes

Masters degrees offered by the institute are classified into two categories: degrees by coursework (M.Tech., M.Mgt., and M.Des.) and degrees by research [M.Tech. (Research)].

The two-year M.Tech. programme is available in almost all engineering departments. Due to stiff competition, one needs a high percentile in the Graduate Aptitude Test in Engineering for admission into this programme. A unique feature of the programmes at the institute is the credit system which allows students to tailor the courses to suit their aptitude, interest and research requirements. Most M.Tech. programmes have a set of hard core courses specified as an essential requirement whereas students can take rest of the credits from many courses available in their parent or other departments and also do a dissertation work on the topic of their choice. These courses attract highly motivated accomplished students, in addition to several sponsored candidates from R&D labs/industries and also from educational institutions under the Quality Improvement Programme.

The Department of Management Studies, one of the oldest management schools in the country (established in 1948), offers a Master of Management programme exclusively for engineering graduates. The Centre for Product Design and Manufacturing offers the Master of Design (M.Des.) course. Started in 1996, the M.Des. programme is a two-year, full-time postgraduate programme.

Bachelors Degree Programmes

An undergraduate programme was conceived, for students who had completed Class XII, during the Centenary Celebrations in 2009. The first batch of students was admitted in 2011. The programme offers a four-year Bachelor of Science (Research) and a five-year integrated Master of Science course in six disciplines: Biology, Chemistry, Environmental Science, Material Science, Mathematics, and Physics. The course aims at exposing the students to the inter-disciplinary nature in which scientific research is done in many upcoming fields, and comes at a time when the importance of science education at the undergraduate level is emphasised and several incentives are provided by the Government to promote the same.

This programme makes the graduates eligible to apply for post-graduate degree programmes in foreign universities, many of which may require 16 years of education before entering a post-graduate degree programme. In India, Bachelor of Science (Research) graduates are eligible to apply for CSIR-NET, a national level examination for securing admission into Ph.D programme into various universities including IISc.

Apart from an intensive training in sciences, courses in Engineering and Humanities are prescribed to empower the student with technical skills required for a scientist, to appreciate the social context as well as constraints of doing science. The science and engineering courses are offered by the respective departments at the Institute; the humanities course is offered by the Centre for Contemporary Studies (CCS) at IISc in collaboration with the Centre for Study of Culture and Society (CSCS), Bengaluru.

Students enrolled in the programme take courses in Biology, Chemistry, Engineering, Humanities, Mathematics, and Physics for the first three semesters which are common and compulsory to all. In the next four semesters, they choose a major discipline of study and take a handful of other science courses and a stipulated number of engineering and humanities courses. The last semester is devoted to a final project. Besides, all the students, either KVPY or DST-Inspire scholars, spend a couple of months in various research institutes across the country exploring a topic or a research problem of their interest.

Admissions Process

Admission to Ph.D programmes of the Institute is based on Graduate Aptitude Test in Engineering (GATE), career records, and technical interviews in the campus. Candidates are called for interviews based on the entrance test of the Institute or GATE or National Eligibility Test. For course oriented degrees, ME and M.Tech, the admission is through GATE, conducted every year. For research-oriented degree M.Tech (Research), the admission is through the GATE. For Master of Management (M.Mgt), which has a ceiling strength of only 25 seats across India, the admission is through Common Admission Test. Admission to M.Des is through the GATE or the Common Entrance Examination for Design. Bachelor of Science graduates can get admission to integrated Ph.D programmes at IISc through the Joint Admission Test for M.Sc. (IIT JAM). IISc does not conduct any entrance test for providing admission. It only organises aptitude test and interview for PG and research courses. The institution offers UG, PG, Research and Ph.D courses in various fields. Admission into these courses is done through JEE Main, JEE Advanced, NEET, CEED, JAM, KVPY and other examinations.

Academic and Industrial Collaborations

The Indian Institute of Science collaborates with various government organisations like the DRDO, the ISRO, Bharat Electronics Limited, Aeronautical Development Agency, National Aerospace Laboratories, CSIR, Department of IT (Government of India), Centre for Development of Advanced Computing, etc. IISc also works in collaboration with private industry and research labs like the Google Inc, General Motors, Microsoft Research, IBM Research, Boeing, Robert Bosch Foundation, Pratt and Whitney and more. A few organisations have been incubated by the Society for Innovation and Development (SID) on campus, including Morphing Machines and S and I, while Gamma Porite is currently under incubation. IISc actively promotes and supports ventures by the faculty, the students and alumni. Strand Life Sciences and Ittiam are some success stories of this initiative.

Indian Institutes of Science Education and Research (IISERs)

The Scientific Advisory Council to the Prime Minister (SAC-PM) under the Chairmanship of Prof. C.N.R. Rao, recommended creation of five new institutions devoted to science education and research to be named "Indian Institutes of Science Education and Research" broadly on the lines of IISc,

Bangalore. Five such Institutes have already been established at Kolkata, Pune, Mohali, Bhopal and Thiruvananthapuram.

The vision of these institutes encompasses creation of research centres of the highest caliber in which teaching and education in basic sciences will be totally integrated with state-of-the-art research. These Institutions are devoted to under-graduate and post-graduate teaching in sciences in an intellectually vibrant atmosphere of research and make education and career in basic sciences more attractive by providing opportunities in integrative teaching and learning of sciences. The goals of these institutes, inter alia, are:

- To create quality education and research in basic sciences.
- To attract and nurture high-quality academic faculty.
- To create integrated Masters Programme in sciences, in order to provide entry into research at a younger age. In addition, the Institutes will have integrated programmes leading to Masters and Ph.Ds to those who hold a Bachelor's degree in science.
- To make possible a flexible borderless curriculum in sciences.
- To actively forge strong relationship with existing universities and colleges and network with laboratories and institutions.
- To establish advanced Research Laboratories and Central facilities.

Admission in undergraduate courses in IISERs is through extended merit list of IIT-Joint Entrance Examination, Kishore Vaigyanik Protsahan Yojana (KVPY) and Direct Admission based on Class X and performance in science stream.

16

Engineering Education

The impulse for creation of centres of technical training came from the British Raj rulers of India. While Superintending Engineers were mostly recruited from Britain, lower grades e.g. Craftsmen, Artisans and Sub-overseers were recruited locally. The necessity to make them more efficient, led to the establishment of industrial schools attached to Indian Ordnance Factories and other engineering establishments.

The first engineering college was established in Madras (now Chennai). A Engineering College in 1847 for the training of Civil Engineers at Roorkee, *Thomason College* (which later became IIT Roorkee) made use of the large workshops and public buildings there that were erected for the Upper Ganges Canal.

In pursuance of the Government policy, three Engineering Colleges were opened by about 1856 in the three Presidencies. In Bengal Presidency, a College called the *Calcutta College of Civil Engineering* (which later became Indian Institute of Engineering Science and Technology, Shibpur) was opened at the Writers' Building in November 1856. In Bombay, Presidency, the *Overseers' School* at Pune eventually became the College of Engineering, Pune and was affiliated to the Bombay University in 1858. In the Madras Presidency, the industrial school attached to the Gun Carriage Factory became ultimately the College of Engineering, Guindy and affiliated to Madras University (1858).

Indian Institutes of Technology

The Indian Institutes of Technology (IITs) has 23 centers located in Bhubaneswar, Bombay, Delhi, Gandhinagar, Guwahati, Hyderabad, Indore, Jodhpur, Kanpur, Kharagpur, Madras, Mandi, Patna, Roorkee, Ropar, Dhanbad, Palakkad, Tirupati, Bhilai, Goa, Jammu, Dharwad, and Varanasi. All IITs enjoy the status of the Institutes of National Importance and are autonomous universities that draft their own curricula. Many IITs are members of LAOTSE, an international network of universities in Europe and Asia. LAOTSE membership allows the IITs to exchange students and senior scholars with universities in other countries.

Admission to undergraduate B.Tech and integrated M.Tech programme are through JEE Advanced (the Joint Entrance Examination Advanced) in which around 150,000 students appear annually out of which only around 11,032 get selected. These 150,000 students are initially sorted out by the JEE Mains (Joint Entrance Examination Mains) which is conducted by the central board (Delhi). Around 1.3 million students appear for this exam. Admission to most postgraduate courses in IITs is granted through various written entrance examinations: GATE (for M.Tech.), JAM (for M.Sc.) and CEED (for M.Des.). The admission for Ph.D. programme is based primarily on a personal interview, though candidates may also have to appear for written tests. The IITs are also well known for their special reservation policy, which is significantly different from the one applied in other educational institutions of India.

National Institutes of Technology

The National Institutes of Technology (NITs) are colleges of engineering and technology education in India. All NITs enjoy the status of the Institutes of National Importance and are autonomous universities that draft their own curricula. They were originally called Regional Engineering Colleges (RECs). In 2002, the Ministry of Human Resource Development, Government of India, decided to upgrade, in phases, all the original 17 RECs as NITs. There are currently 31 NITs, with the inception of 10 new NITs in the year 2010 and another in 2015. The 31 NITs are located in Allahabad, Agartala, Bhopal, Durgapur, Hamirpur, Kozhikode, Kurukshetra, Jalandhar, Jamshedpur, Jaipur, Nagpur, Patna, Raipur, Rourkela, Silchar, Srinagar, Surathkal, Surat, Tiruchirappalli, Warangal, Yupia, New Delhi, Farmagudi, Imphal, Shillong, Aizawl, Dimapur, Karaikal, Ravangla, Srinagar and Tadepalligudem. The Government of India has introduced the National Institutes of Technology (NIT) Act 2010 to bring 31 such institutions within the ambit of the Act and to provide them with complete autonomy in their functioning. The NITs are deliberately scattered throughout the country in line with the government norm of an NIT in every major state of India to promote regional development. The individual NITs, after the introduction of the NIT Act, have been functioning as autonomous technical universities and hence can draft their own curriculum and functioning policies.

The admission to undergraduate programmes of all the NITs was done by the All India Engineering Entrance Examination popularly known as AIEEE. From the year 2013, AIEEE was replaced by JEE-Main (Joint Entrance Examination–Main) in which 40 per cent weightage is given to the Higher Secondary results and 60 per cent (as per new rules the weightage of marks in board has been changed and HS board percentage is not counted) weightage given to the JEE (Main) results. The examination is objective by nature and is conducted by the Central Board of Secondary Education (CBSE). More than fourteen lakh (1,400,000) applicants took part in 2013 for approximately 15,500 seats in the B.Tech and B.Arch programmes available in all the NITs put together.

Indian Institutes of Engineering Science and Technology

Indian Institutes of Engineering Science and Technology (abbreviated assists) are a group of academic institutions in India for research and education in engineering. These were originally proposed by the Government of India in 2007 to meet the increasing demand for technological and scientific workforce in the industrial and service sectors of India as well as the growing need for qualified personnel in research and development. It was decided that the institutes under the banner of IIEST were to be created by upgrading existing engineering colleges or universities under the various State governments of India through an Act of the Parliament of India, instead of founding completely new institutes. After upgrading, these institutes would also be granted the status of "Institutes of National Importance (INI)". The first institute to be upgraded to IIEST was Bengal Engineering and Science University, Shibpur, which was a university under the Government of West Bengal prior to the upgrade process.

Indian Institutes of Information Technology

Indian Institutes of Information Technology (IIITs) are a group of four institutes of higher education in India, focused on information technology. They are established by the Central Government, centrally funded, and managed by the Ministry of Human Resource Development.

The Institution of Engineers (India)

AMIE was established in 1920 in Calcutta (Kolkata), West Bengal and is acclaimed to have pioneered non-formal education in Engineering. IEI(I) conducts an examination for its Associate Membership (AMIE). This examination is considered to be on par with B.E./B.Tech when contemplated as an eligibility qualification to write competitive examinations like the Indian Civil Service, Indian Engineering Services, GATE, etc., and for employment in Government, public and private sectors in India. This qualification is recognised by Ministry of HRD, Government of India as equivalent to B.E./B.Tech.

Polytechnic Institutes

In India there are institutions which offer three year diploma in engineering post-tenth class. These institutes have affiliation from state board of technical education of respective state governments. After completion one can apply for post of junior engineer or continue higher studies by appearing for exams of AMIE to become an engineering graduate. Some of these are:

- Dr. B.R. Ambedkar Institute of Technology
- Calcutta Technical School, Kolkata
- Jnan Chandra Ghosh Polytechnic, Kolkata
- Sai Polytechnic College, Sri Sai University, Palampur, Pathankot, Amritsar
- Pusa Polytechnic (being one of the famous Polytechnic in India)
- Government Girls Polytechnic, Bilaspur
- Government Polytechnic, Ambikapur
- Government Polytechnic, Korba
- Government Polytechnic, Mumbai
- Government Polytechnic, Lucknow
- Government Polytechnic, Nainital
- Government Polytechnic, Nilokheri
- Government Polytechnic, Barabanki
- Government Polytechnic, Nagpur
- Government Polytechnic, Anantnag, Jammu & Kashmir
- Government Polytechnic, Solapur
- Kirodimal Government Polytechnic, Raigarh

17
Space Technology

The space research activities in India were imitated during the early 1960s, when applications using satellites were in experimental stages even in the USA. With the live transmission of Tokyo Olympic Games across the pacific by the American Satellite 'syncom–3' demonstrating the power of Communication satellites.

Dr. Vikram Sarabhai, the founding father of India Space Programme, quickly recognised the benefits of space technologies for India.

As a first step, the Department of Atomic Energy formed the Indian National Committee for Space Research under the leadership of Dr. Sarabhai and Ramanathan in 1962. The Indian Space Research Organisation (ISRO) was later formed on 15 August 1969. The prime objective of ISRO is to develop space technology and its application to various national needs. It is one of the largest space agencies in the world. The Department of Space Commission was setup in 1972 and ISRO was brought under DoS on 1 June 1972.

Since inception, the Indian space programme has been orchestrated well and had three distinct elements such as satellites for communication and remote sensing, the space transportation system and application programmes. Two major operational systems have been established—the Indian National Satellite (INSAT) for telecommunication, television broadcasting and meteorological services and the Indian Remote Satellite (IRS) for monitoring and management of natural resources and Distance Management Support.

The first of the Indian Regional Navigational Satellite System (IRNSS-1A) has been successfully launched in July 2013. The years ahead with witness the completion of the IRNSS constellation with seven satellites leading to the introduction of satellite-based positioning and timing services in the country.

New capabilities in Earth Observations were planned with the development of Geo imaging Satellite (GISAT) to provide near real time images of large areas of the country and hyper spectral imaging systems for natural resources survey and disaster management applications.

Several exciting missions in Space Science and Planetary Exploration have been planned near future including Chandrayaan-2, with a lander and a rover intended for in-situ investigations of the Lunar Surface; multi-wavelength Astronomy observatory satellite ASTROSAT-1 for observation of celestial objects covering optical, UV and X-ray bands and India's first space- borne solar coronagraph mission ADITYA-1 for studies on coronal mass ejections.

1. Space Capsule Recovery

A leap-frog in Indian Launch Vehicle Technology was achieved in 2007 through the Space Capsule Recovery Experiment Mission SRE-1 which established India's technological capability to recover an orbiting satellite with precise re-entry trajectories.

2. Mars Orbiter Mission

India's first inter planetary mission, the Mars Orbiter Spacecraft was successfully launched on 5 November 2013 onboard PSLV-C25. The voyage of the spacecraft towards Mars, following crucial orbital manoeuvre of Trans-Mars Injection on 1 December 2013, made India to become one of the four nations in the world to send space mission to Planet Mars. Mars Orbiter Mission is mainly intended to establish the Indian technological capability to reach Martian orbit and to explore Mars surface features, morphology, mineralogy and Martian atmosphere by indigenous scientific instruments.

3. PSLV—A Workhorse Launch Vehicle

India's Polar Satellite Launch Vehicle (PSLV), with a proven track record of 24 successful flights, has provided the country the crucial autonomy in 'access to space'. During the last decade, PSLV had 15 successively successful flights and has placed 23 Indian satellites and 31 foreign satellites into orbit. The versatile vehicle PSLV has been successfully used for launching lighter communication and navigation satellites into GTO, apart from launching remote sensing satellites to Low Earth Orbit and Interplanetary missions. PSLV, to its credit, has the successful launch of India's first Inter-planetary Mission to Mars in November 2013 as well India's first Lunar Mission Chandrayaan-1 earlier in September 2008.

4. India's Mission to Moon

India's maiden moon exploration mission 'Chandrayaan-1' was launched in October 2008 for mapping the lunar surface with high resolution remote sensing and study the chemical and mineralogical composition. This mission has enabled to detect the presence of Hydroxyl (OH), a molecule consisting of oxygen and hydrogen atoms and water molecules on the lunar surface, which has set new directions of lunar explorations in the global community.

5. Indian Cryogenic Engine and Stage and GSLV–D5

The successful flight testing of indigenous cryogenic stage onboard GSLV-D5 Flight on 5 January 2014. Geosynchronous Satellite Launch Vehicle (GSLV) is capable of placing two tonne class communication satellite into Geosynchronous Transfer Orbit (GTO) and India is one among six countries in the world to demonstrate such launch capability to GTO with the use of complex cryogenic technology.

6. Remote Sensing and National Natural Resource Management System

The Indian Remote Sensing Satellites (IRS) System, with currently 11 satellites in orbit, is one of the largest constellations of remote sensing satellites in operation in the world today. It provides inputs for management of natural resources and various developmental projects across the country using space based imagery.

During the last decade, 13 remote sensing satellites have been launched and operationalised. The imaging technology of the country witnessed a quantum jump with the successful launch of Radar Imaging Satellite (RISAT-1) in 2012. RISAT-1 gave the all-weather day and night imaging capability for the country, crucial for applications in Agriculture and Disaster Management. The advanced cartography satellite, Cartosat-2 launched in 2007, enhanced the imaging capability to sub-metre high resolution in tune with the global trend and provided immense services for cartographic applications. To study the climate of tropical regions, a joint Indo-France satellite Megha-Tropiques was launched in October 2011. With the launch of advanced meteorological satellite INSAT-3D in July 2013, an atmospheric sounder payload has been placed over the Indian Ocean for the first time which enabled detailed climatic studies over this region. Data from IRS satellites are used for meeting varieties of societal needs—locating sources of drinking water in remote areas, potential fishing zone advisories, environmental monitoring, agricultural crop forecasting, disaster management—to name a few.

7. International Co-operation

India's maiden mission to moon Chandrayaan-1 carried six scientific instruments from USA and Europe. Two satellite missions viz. Megha-Tropiques and SARAL (Satellite with ARgos and ALtica) were realised through India-France Co-operation. YouthSat, a satellite for space weather studies has been realised by young scientists of India and Russia. India has co-operation with Jet Propulsion Laboratory of USA for ground stations support for Mars Orbiter Mission and India and USA together are planning to develop a dual band Radar Imaging Satellite to be launched by 2019-2020.

8. INSAT System

INSAT system has grown as one of the largest domestic communications satellite constellations in the Asian region. In the last decade, INSAT system has been augmented with the launch of 12 INSAT/GSAT communication satellites. A vital application of INSAT system in the last decade has been in the field of education with the launch of thematic satellite EDUSAT in 2004. EDUSAT was specially designed to spread education (formal and informal) at all levels and regions of the country. INSAT system was also instrumental in taking the benefits of space technology to the doorsteps of common man through the initiatives of Tele-medicine and Village Resource Centres in the country.

9. Satellite Navigation

India is pursuing satellite navigation programme to provide position and navigation information for various applications. Indian Regional Navigation Satellite System (IRNSS) is being developed to provide accurate position information service to users in India as well as the region extending up to 1500 kms from its boundary. The first satellite of this 7-satellite constellation, IRNSS 1A was successfully launched in July 2013. In addition ISRO and Airports Authority of India have jointly taken up GPS Aided Geo Augmented Navigation (GAGAN) programme, as a forerunner for the operational Satellite based Augmentation System (SBAS) over the Indian Airspace. GAGAN payloads are already incorporated in GSAT 8 and GSAT 10 satellites.

10. Space Commerce/Antrix

As the commercial and marketing arm of ISRO, Antrix is engaged in providing Space products and services to international customers worldwide. By using the launch services of ISRO's workhorse launch vehicle, PSLV, 31 satellites belonging to 17 countries have been launched on commercial terms during the last 10 years. Additionally, the data from Indian Remote sensing satellites are commercially disseminated to users globally.

Indian Space Research Organisation (ISRO)

Indian Space Organisation (ISRO) is the space agency of the Government of India headquartered in the city of Bangalore. Its vision is to harness space technology for national development while pursuing space science research and planetary exploration.

Formed in 1969, ISRO superseded the erstwhile 'Indian National Committee for space research established in 1962 by the efforts of Jawaharlal Nehru, India's first Prime Minister and his close aids and scientist Vikram Sarabhai. It's managed by the Department of Space which reports to the Prime Minister.

ISRO built India's first satellite, Aryabhatta, which was launched on 19 April 1975 by the Soviet Union. It was named after the Mathematician Aryabhatta. In 1980, Rohini became the first satellite to be placed in orbit by an Indian made launch vehicle, SLV-3. ISRO subsequently developed two other rockets, the Polar Launch Vehicle (PSLV) for launching satellites into polar orbits and the Geosyn chronous Satellite Launch Vehicle (GSLV) for placing satellite into geo satellite orbits. These rockets have launched numerous communication satellites and earth's observation satellites. Satellites navigation systems like GAGAN and IRNSS have been deployed in January 2014.

ISRO sent a lunar orbiter. Chandrayaan-1, on 22 October 2008 and a Mars orbiter, Mission on 5 November 2013, which entered Mars orbit on 24 September 2014, making India the first nation to succeed on its first attempt to Mars, and ISRO the fourth space agency in the world as well as the first space agency in Asia to reach Mars orbit. On 18 June 2016 ISRO set a record with a launch of 20 satellites in a single payload, one being a satellite from Google. On 15 February 2017, ISRO launched 104 satellites in a single rocket (PSLV-cgy) and created a world record.

ISRO launched its heaviest rockets, Geosynchronous Satellite Launch Vehicle-Mars-III (GSLV-MK III) on 5 June 2017 and placed a communication satellite GST-19 in orbit. With this launch, ISRO became capable of launching four-tonne heavy satellite. Further plan include the development of Unified Launch Vehicle, development of a reusable launch vehicle, human space flight, controlled soft lunar landing, interplanetary probes and a solar spacecraft mission.

The prime objective of ISRO is to use space technology and its application to various national tasks. The Indian Space programme was driven by the Vision of Vikram Sarabhai. As he said "There are some who question the relevance of space activities in a developing nation. To us, there is no ambiguity of purpose. We do not have the fantasy of competing with the economically advanced nations in the exploration of the Moon or the planets or manned spaceflight. But we are convinced that if we are to play a meaningful role nationally, and in the community of nations, we must be second to none in the application of advanced technologies to the real problems of man and society.

Organisational Structure and Facilities

ISRO is managed by the Department of Space of the Government of India (DoS). DoS itself falls under the authority of the Prime Minister office and the Space Commission, and manages the following agencies and institutes:

Indian Space Research Organisation

- Vikram Sarabhai Space Centre (VSSC), Thiruvananthapuram.
- Liquid Propulsion Systems Centre (LPSC), Thiruvananthapuram.
- Satish Dhawan Space Centre (SDSC-SHAR), Sriharikota.
- ISRO Propulsion Complex (IPRC), Mehendragiri.
- ISRO Satellite Centre (ISAC), Bangalore.
- Space Applications Centre (SAC), Ahmedabad.
- National Remote Sensing Centre (NRSC), Hyderabad.
- ISRO Inertial Systems Unit (IISU), Thiruvananthapuram.
- Development and Educational Communication Unit (DECU), Ahmedabad.
- Master Control Facility (MCF), Hassan, Karnataka.
- ISRO Telemetry, Tracking and Command Network (ISTRAC), Bangalore.
- Laboratory for Electro-Optics Systems (LEOS), Bangalore.
- Indian Institute of Remote Sensing (IIRS), Dehradun.
- Antrix Corporation the marketing arm of ISRO, Bangalore.
- Physical Research Laboratory (PRL), Ahmedabad.
- National Atmospheric Research Laboratory (NARL), Gadanki, Andhra Pradesh.
- North-Eastern Space Applications Centre (NE-SAC), Umiam.
- Semi-Conductor Laboratory (SCL), Mohali.
- Indian Institute of Space Science and Technology (IIST), Thiruvananthapuram—India's space university.

Research Facilities

Facility	*Location*
Vikram Sarabhai Space Centre	Thiruvananthapuram
Liquid Propulsion Systems Centre	Thiruvananthapuram and Bangalore
Physical Research Laboratory	Ahmedabad
Semi-Conductor Laboratory	Chandigarh
National Atmospheric Research Laboratory	Tirupati
Space Applications Centre	Ahmedabad
North-Eastern Space Applications Centre	Shillong

Test Facilities

Facility	*Location*
ISRO Propulsion Complex	Mahendragiri

Construction and Launch Facilities

Facility	*Location*
ISRO Satellite Centre	Bangalore
Laboratory for Electro-Optics Systems	Bangalore
Satish Dhawan Space Centre	Sriharikota
Thumba Equatorial Rocket Launching Station	Thiruvananthapuram

Tracking and Control Facilities

Facility	*Location*
Indian Deep Space Network (IDSN)	Bangalore
National Remote Sensing Centre	Hyderabad
ISRO Telemetry, Tracking and Command Network	Bangalore (headquarters) and a number of ground stations throughout India and World
Master Control Facility	Bhopal; Hassan

Human Resource Development

Facility	*Location*
Indian Institute of Remote Sensing (IIRS)	Dehradun
Indian Institute of Space Science and Technology (IIST)	Thiruvananthapuram
Development and Educational Communication Unit	Ahmedabad

Other Facilities

- Balasore Rocket Launching Station (BRLS)—Odisha
- ISRO Inertial Systems Unit (IISU)—Thiruvananthapuram
- Indian Regional Navigational Satellite System (IRNSS)
- Aerospace Command of India (ACI)
- Indian National Committee for Space Research (INCOSPAR)

- Inter University Centre for Astronomy and Astrophysics (IUCAA)
- Indian Space Science Data Centre (ISSDC)
- Spacecraft Control Centre (SCC)
- Regional Remote Sensing Service Centres (RRSSC)
- Development and Educational Communication Unit (DECU)
- National Deep Space Observation Centre (NDSPO)

Launch Vehicle Fleet

- Satellite Launch Vehicle (SLV)
- Augmented Satellite Launch Vehicle (ASLV)
- Geosynchronous Satellite Launch Vehicle (GSLV)
- Geosynchronous Satellite Launch Vehicle Mark-III (GSLV III)

Satellite Programmes

- INSAT Series
- The IRS Series
- Radar Imaging Satellites
- South Asia Satellite
- Gagan Satellite Navigation System
- IRNSS Satellite Navigation System

Human Spaceflight Programme

- Technology Demonstration
- Astronaut and other facilities
- Crewed Spacecraft

Planetary Sciences and Astronomy

- Astronaut

Extraterrestrial Exploration

- Lunar: Chandrayaan-1
- Mars Orbiter Mission

Future Projects

Forthcoming Satellites

Satellite Name	*Notes*
GSAT-11	GSAT-11 is based on I-6K bus, which is under advanced stage of development. The spacecraft can generate 10–12 KW of power and can

(*Contd.*)

Satellite Name	Notes
	support payload power of 8 KW. The payload configuration is on-going. It consists of 16 spot beams covering entire country including Andaman and Nicobar Islands. The communication link to the user-end terminals operates in Ku-band while the communication link to the hubs operates in Ka-band. The payload is configured to be operated as a high data throughput satellite, to be realised in orbit in 2018.
GSAT-30	It is expected to be launched from French arianespace in 2019.
GSAT-31	It is expected to be launched from French arianespace in 2019.
GISAT 1	Geospatial imagery to facilitate continuous observation of Indian sub-continent, quick monitoring of natural hazards and disaster.
NISAR	NASA-ISRO Synthetic Aperture Radar (Nisar) is a joint project between NASA and ISRO to co-develop and launch a dual frequency synthetic aperture radar satellite to be used for remote sensing. It is notable for being the first dual band radar imaging satellite.

Future Extraterrestrial Exploration

ISRO's missions beyond Earth's orbit include Chandrayaan-1 (to the Moon) and Mars Orbiter Mission (to Mars). ISRO plans to follow up with Chandrayaan-2, Mars Orbiter Mission 2, and is assessing missions to Venus, the Sun, and near-Earth objects such as asteroids and comets.

Destination	*Craft name*	*Launch vehicle*	*Year*
Moon	Chandrayaan-2	GSLV III	2019
Sun	Aditya-L1	PSLV-XL	2021
Mars	Mars Orbiter Mission 2 (Mangalyaan 2)	GSLV III	2021-22
Venus	Indian Venusian Orbiter Mission	PSLV-XL	2023
Jupiter	TBD		

Chandrayaan-2

Chandrayaan-2 will be India's second mission to the Moon, which will include an orbiter and lander-rover module. Chandrayaan-2 will be launched on India's Geosynchronous Satellite Launch Vehicle Mark III (GSLV-MkIII) in 2019. The science goals of the mission are to further improve the understanding of the origin and evolution of the Moon.

Mars Orbiter Mission 2

The next Mars mission, Mars Orbiter Mission 2, also called Mangalyaan 2, will likely be launched in 2021 or 2022. It will have a less elliptical orbit around Mars and could weigh seven times more than the first mission. This orbiter mission will facilitate scientific community to address the open science problems. The science payload of the proposed satellite is likely to be 100 kg.

Solar Orbiter

ISRO plans to carry out a mission to the Sun by the year 2019–20. The probe is named Aditya-1 and will weigh about 400 kg. It is the first Indian space-based solar coronagraph to study the corona in visible and near-IR bands. Launch of the Aditya mission was planned during the heightened solar activity period in 2012, but was postponed to 2019–20 due to the extensive work involved in the fabrication, and other technical aspects. The main objective of the mission is to study coronal mass ejections (CMEs), their properties (the structure and evolution of their magnetic fields for example), and consequently constrain parameters that affect space weather.

Venus and Jupiter

The ISRO is in the process of conducting conceptual studies that could take up to two years before deciding on a plan to send a spacecraft to Jupiter or Venus.

Applications

- Telecommunication
- Resource Management
- Military
- Academic
- Telemedicine
- Biodiversity Information System
- Cartography

18
Science Education

Science Education in Post-Independent India

In the post independent India, our constitution adopted the goals of establishing the society based on the scientific temper, humanism and spirit of inquiry. It enshrines in Article 51A(h) of the constitution that it is the fundamental duty of the every citizen of the country to inculcate, propagate and further disseminate the scientific temper in society. In fact, India is the only country in the world that has adopted such obligation in the written constitution.

Science education policy in India is based on the recognition that scientific thinking is the cherished values of human efforts, yearning, and struggles against the culture of fear and limitations. It is as precious as society itself for the advancement of society towards social progressivism to achieve the goals of social, moral and spiritual values and material wellbeing. However, in the recent decades, it has been seen that there is a retreat of public reasoning in the public sphere that has helped in the culmination and rise of anti-science attitude and religious revivalism in public life (Raina, 2016). This poses a great challenge to the society. In 1981 "A Statement on Scientific Temper," was endorsed by Nehru Centre assuming that scientific inquiry helps people to form and develop their idea and argument based on proof and evidence rather than mundane reasons that would finally negate the prevailing obscurantism and superstitions in the society.

National Council Education Research and Training (NCERT) Position Paper on science has recognised that our science textbooks are overloaded with scientific facts. It also mentions that science teaching in India suffers from the problems like:

(a) It is lagging behind in achieving enshrined values like humanism, scientific temper and social justice in our constitution;
(b) Science education, even at its best, does not encourage inventiveness and creativity;

(c) Overpowering examination system is the fundamental problems of science education.

Similar conclusions have been also drawn by Aikenhead. According to Aikenhead, students are increasingly disenchanted with the content of school science. School science is full of content which is socially sterile, intellectually boring, and dismissive of student's life. It is no wonder that most students do not able to make meanings out of classroom teaching of science and not able to correlate with what is being taught in the classroom with their personal life. This has proved fatal for the development popularity of science as a subject among students and promoted the myth of science as a brainy and difficult subject. In the similar vein Sarangapani laments the pathetic condition of the way in which science is being taught in the classrooms. According to her as a country we may take pride in the success of science graduate student abroad but we have failed to take the question of the seriousness of science teaching and learning in the classrooms. Among other problems, she counts, is the authoritarian approach of teaching science in India that hardly allows autonomy to learners and teachers. It adheres to absolute and strict interpretation of textbooks in the classrooms. Kumar called it preponderance of the Textbook Culture. Sarangapani traced out the roots of such outdated monolithic culture of learning in the colonial origin of the education system. According to Mukherjee, in spite of the tremendous socio-political odds, the success of Raman, Saha and Bose has triggered a sense of pride and jubilance among the Indian people. In 1961, a committee namely Indian parliamentary and scientific committee was formed under the leadership of Late Shri Lal Bahadur Shastri to find out the problems facing science school in Indian school system. The other problems which were taken for serious consideration were finding out the relationship between central and state government policies regarding science education policies and exploring the courses offered in the different schools under different state educational system. In 1964, Indian Education Commission under the chair of Dr. Kothari pointed out that the state of science in India is in pathetic condition and system has failed to reckon with the explosion of knowledge in science. In order to meet this immediate challenge, it was recommended that projects should be conducted to upgrade school curriculum and textbooks. In 1968, a National Policy of Education (NPE) was launched with the aim to connect the development of the nation, citizenship education and science education. It laid stress on social reconstruction and also on mitigating regional imbalances in the development of educational system. In 1986, NPE prioritised the agendas of inclusive education, vocational training, technical and professional education and laid stress on reducing female illiteracy in the country. In this way, educational policy was linked to the spread of scientific literacy and scientific awareness in the society that acted to stimulate the different education subsystem to produce skilled workforce needed for the economy. But in this process of production of scientific workforce for the industrial purposes encompasses the darker side. It came as a heavy burden to students at large. Textbooks were overloaded with more and more factual information. Reforms were often done on episodic basis to add more information citing the reason like information explosion. This phenomenon and ideology has been analysed by famous Canadian science educator Aiken head who has called it the pipeline production.

In 1970s, science educators, independent resource groups, and educationists collectively came together to challenge the orthodoxy of Indian school science and pitched in for formulating an approach that contextualises science education from the learner's centered perspective. Hoshangabad Science Teaching Programme (HSTP) was one such programme that was started in 1972 in Hoshangabad district of Madhya Pradesh province of India. The experiences of Hoshangabad Science Teaching Programme suggested changing the perspective on science teaching in India. HSTP advocated that country needs a fresh restart to develop a science The State of Science Education in Post-Independent India: education teaching paradigm and for that science educator, teacher and civil society as a whole have to think outside the box solution. Although closed, HSTP took pride in the fact that innovative concepts like learning by discovery methods, inquiry method, etc. are not only included in the latest policy documents at the national level but also emphasised to practice within the classrooms. Similar efforts of curriculum making were taken in other countries like in the United Kingdom in Nuffield Reforms, and in U.S. National Science Foundation.

In 1975, NCERT in the framework of the curricular objectives has laid down the objectives of education. NCERT defined curriculum as the sum total of all the deliberately planned set of educational experiences provided to the child by the school. Kala and Ramadas reviewed these trends in science curriculum reforms research that have occurred worldwide. According to them, Piaget's influences in the domain of science education reforms led to a shift from behaviourism to constructivism and by the 1970s, the major trends in science education research shifted from constructivism to philosophy of science. Philosophy of science, specifically the work of Popper, Kuhn and Lakatos started to find currency in the domain of science education worldwide. Ideas such as theory-laden observations, nature of scientific inquiry started to impinge in the school curriculum theories and texts. They explained that justification for applying ideas from the philosophy of science to science education can be found in the child as scientist metaphor, which had been subtly present since Piaget. Since child could be considered as a novice scientist, researchers in science education thought that philosophy of science, which attempted to lay down the foundations for science, could similarly be used to interpret children's conceptions of science and provide guidelines for interpreting children's conceptions of science. Confrey pointed out that philosophy of science allows researchers to critique the underlying inductive conception of science which has permeated science textbooks in the form of the scientific method. However, Kala and Ramadas contend that unfortunately in the practices of science education research and curriculum making these developments in domain independent science education research like epistemology studies, cognitive psychology is still to be seen in India.

New Science Education and Curriculum

With the upcoming of 21st century the world has witnessed unprecedented socio-economic changes due to explosion in information technology and the process of socio-political and economic integration that necessitated the agendas of reforming the curriculum. The aims of science curriculum reforms across the cultures have been to help students to develop informed and enriching understanding of science and promote science learning as joyous experience that promote critical and creative thinking through various innovative methods like learning by doing, learning by inquiry method, and discovery method.

This is the departure from the old ways of knowing science in schools that only inscribes science teaching by giving instructions that students in the classrooms and school followed to mime and mimic the scientific process. The recognition of the fact that scientific knowledge does not only entail knowledge of products of science but science learning is all about learning processes, cultures and practices of science is important from the educational praxis point of view that emphasises the bridging the gap between theory and practice. Science learning does include knowing methods, scientific practices of scientists and nature of science. In other words how does scientific knowledge emerge is important to know for student's comprehensive and deeper understanding of scientific knowledge? These episteme values also include questions like what demarcates science from other way of knowing like religion and philosophy. Allchin's has called it knowing the whole conceptualisation of science rather than processed image of science that is currently filters in textbooks. It adopts and hence prescribes the image of science that is reductionist. Adopting the whole conceptualisation of science in accordance with the nature of science can be a good starting point to renew the energy that is needed to review of science education curriculum to get benefit from the pedagogical analysis of teaching science. More particularly the idea of teaching of science and about science extracting from philosophy and methodology of science and science studies may work wonder to kill the symptomatic culture of monolithic way of teaching content of science and extrinsic learning of students which is present in today's day education system.

Conclusion

National Curriculum Framework Policy (NCF) 2005 of India recommends teaching science as a process/inquiry and value system. It talks about maintaining the cognitive validity, process validity, historical validity, environmental validity, and ethical validity in science textbooks. But unfortunately, today's science textbook hardly takes cognisance of such issues. It projects the image of science that is empty of the epistemic, cognitive and social values of science. Consequently, as it is the case the overwhelming majority of students ascribe the naive conception of science and teachers continue to structure their science argument in a way that is incommensurate with how scientist proceed to scientific activities, scientific deliberations, and unpack their inquiries into natural phenomena in real life situation.

The State of Science Education in Post-Independent India: The understanding of science as a dynamic enterprise human activities consisting of socio-psycho values that mediates within scientific communities helps learner to situate the scientific knowledge in the real context of social world. The need to apply scientific knowledge in the real life examples like socio-scientific complexities of personal and public issues in society has gained ground. There is increasing importance of pedagogical innovation of teaching science in the classroom that requires: (a) teaching nature of science along with the content of science; (b) the knowledge of how science is manufactured including the contribution of affective side of human like role socio-psycho effects like creativity and errors. Such a system of pedagogical analysis of teaching science has been enriched by disciplines like History, Philosophy and Sociology of Science (HPSS) that makes complimentary conversation with science education and presents the Nature of Science in brief form to adopt it in science curriculum. Reforms in science curriculum are also necessitated to disseminate scientific temper as the dominant mode of thinking in a society that helps people to base their reasoning on the cause-effect relationship. In fact, scientific thinking that favours the value-system supported by egalitarian, secular, and rational values and promotes the development of the collective conscience of the society based on the spirit of inquiry is accepted on the basis of the right to question and be questioned. It involves knowing the grammar of science so that people can apply it to many aspects of life ranging from ethics to politics to economics.

Usefulness of science to society:

- Science produces more responsible citizens. Science helps to build a strong economy. Science contributes to global health.
- Science contributes to an informed decisions that impact the world. Science ensures future support of scientific research and advancements.
- Science improves the quality of daily life, underpins prosperity and increases our readiness to face the challenges of the future. Science helps us to become an Innovative Nation.
- Science will help us to address the main challenges we face as a nation and as a planet:
  - Tackling and adapting to climate change.
  - Global security and international terrorism.
  - Rising population and the consequent pressure on food, water and other natural resources.

While there is no doubt that there never had been better time than today in the recorded history to pursue science in India, the challenge is to secure the future. Planning for future is more challenging now than in 1950s. At that time, the options were limited due to scarcity of resources. Very small number of trained manpower was available to steer the country's education initiatives. Now, very large number of accomplished scientists and technocrats are available to pursue a number of options to meet the aspirations of the people. It may sound cliché. India is a country of enormous diversity. No single model of science education and research would cater to the needs and aspirations of the entire nation. Still, a consensus seems to have emerged on the need to integrate high quality research with undergraduate teaching to improve science education in India and to enhance the number and quality of future academic as well as industrial researchers in the country. By dedicating certain amount of time for teaching, faculty is also expected to improve the quality of their research.

Since the beginning of this century, several new initiatives are being explored such as:

(i) Establishment of large number of broad education centres—Central Universities, IISERs, NISER, IITs, NIPERs.

(ii) Establishment of specialised centres of research and education in space technology, defence technology, translational research, biotechnology and stem cell biology.

(iii) Expansion of existing institutes such as IITs, IISc and TIFR. The latter two would soon be initiating undergraduate education programmes.

Only time will tell what would be the outcome of these initiatives.

Most decisions in historical contexts would look either very good or bad, but at the time of making the decisions, we would be dabbling with only hypothetical situations. Any decision would be based on some logical thinking that suggests that a particular hypothetical scenario would be better than the other hypothetical one. Here, we could learn something from evolution. More the genetic diversity better the chances that a species survives and proliferates. This is because we could always find few individuals carrying genetic variants that would help them to adapt (better than their ancestral population) to a new environment. This is precisely what we need to do. Wiser the nation if it invests on a broad-based education system, which nurtures both curiosity and creativity amongst its citizens. Such education system would create amongst the people the skills and competence in diverse fields and thereby improves the overall preparedness of the country in the long run.

Irrespective of diversity in the opinion on what and how to research and teach, there is no argument that on the three conceptual foundations, on which any scientific enterprise should be built.

(i) *Strong emphasis on basic science:* When it comes to science, "no national scientific enterprise can be sustainable in the long term if it does not contain generous room for curiosity-driven research. While the technological outcomes and social benefits of basic science are almost always long-term and rarely predictable, such science creates and consolidates overall competence and intellectual diversity".

(ii) *Excellent academic ambiance:* Success of any creative endeavour is dependent on large number of excellent people working in the same organisation. This creates a threshold level of academic excellence and provides necessary forum for cross-fertilisation of ideas, internal collaborations and unbiased internal criticism. A critical level of academic excellence is also necessary to pursue bigger questions in science, most of which would require interdisciplinary efforts. If we read the history of most academic places in India and other countries, an ambiance described above has been the foundation for success. Only way to create such an ambiance is by carefully choosing faculty for their research accomplishments, promise, teaching proficiency and mentoring abilities. Ideally, faculty should have the ability and courage to challenge dogmas, inculcate concepts of scientific and mathematical inquiry in their research and teaching and promote critical thinking and reasoning amongst their students. Equally important is to ensure that our faculty upholds highest standards of integrity and ethics in their professional and personal life.

(iii) *Free and fair organisational system:* Academic freedom, a democratic and consultative administrative set up, unbiased periodic review of performance and strict accountability to the support provided are equally important for maintaining highest standards of academic excellence.

Landmarks in the Development of Science Education in India

The important landmarks in the development of science education are the following:

Report of the Secondary Education Commission (1953)

- Science is the basic component of education and culture; so it should be made an integral part of school education.
- The present society is the science-based society. The present century has made tremendous advancement in scientific and technical knowledge as a result of explosion of knowledge. In such a situation one of the main functions of education is to keep pace with this advancement of knowledge. Another feature of modern society is the rapid social change. In the situation of change, the school must always be alert if it is to keep abreast of significant changes. An education system which does not renovate itself continuously becomes out-dated and puts hindrance to progress. To keep pace with modernisation the IEC is of the opinion that "greater emphasis must be placed on vocational subjects, science education and research".

All India Seminars on Teaching Science (1956)

The seminar held at Tara Devi in 1956 made serious discussions on almost all the aspects concerning the teaching of science in schools. It had suggested a unique and uniform system of science teaching.

Arousing and maintaining interest in nature and the physical and social environments; arousing love for nature and the habit of conserving nature and its resources.

I. Developing the habit of observation, exploration, classification and systematic way of thinking.
II. Developing the child's power of manipulation and creative and inventive faculties.
III. Developing neat and orderly habits.
IV. Inculcation of habits of healthful living.

In addition to the above the following aims and objective are suitable of inclusion at the middle school level:

I. Provision of information concerning nature and science which may serve as the basis for a general science course at the higher secondary level.

II. Developing the ability to reach generalisations and to apply them for solving everyday problems.

III. Understanding the impact of science upon our way of living.

IV. Developing interest in scientific hobbies.

V. Inspiring children "by stories about scientists and their discoveries and inventions.

National Scientific Policy Resolution (1958)

It envisaged the cultivation of science and scientific research in all its aspects. Its recommendations are as follow:

1. The key to national prosperity, apart from the spirit of the people, lies, in the modern age, in the effective combination of three factors, technology, raw materials and capital, of which the first is perhaps the most important, since the creation and adoption of new scientific techniques can, in fact, make up for a deficiency in natural resources, and reduce the demands on capital. But technology can only grow out of the study of science and its applications.
2. The dominating feature of the contemporary world is the intense cultivation of science on a large scale, a standard of living and social and cultural amenities, which were once confined to a very small privileged minority of the population. Science has led to the growth and diffusion of culture to an extent never possible before.
3. It is only through the scientific approach and method and the use of scientific knowledge that reasonable material and cultural amenities and services can be provided for every member of the community, and it is out of recognition of this possibility that the idea of a welfare state has grown.
4. The wealth and prosperity of nation depend on the effective utilisation of its human and material resources through industrialisation. The use of human material for industrialisation demands its education in science and training in technical skills.
5. Science and technology can make up for deficiencies in raw materials by providing substitutes, or, indeed, by providing skills which can be exported in return for raw materials.
6. Science has developed at an ever-increasing pace since the beginning of the century, so that the gap between the advanced and backward countries has widened more and more. It is only by adopting the most vigorous measures and by putting forward our utmost effort into the development of science that we can bridge the gap.

7. The Government of India have accordingly decided that the aims of their scientific policy will be:
   - to foster, promote, and sustain, by all appropriate means, the cultivation of science, and scientific research in all its aspects pure, applied, and educational;
   - to ensure an adequate supply, within the country, of research scientists of the highest quality, and to recognise their work as an important component of the strength of the nation;
   - to encourage, and initiate, with all possible speed, programmes for the training of scientific and technical personnel;
   - to ensure that the creative talent of men and women is encouraged and finds full scope in scientific activity;
   - to encourage individual initiative for the acquisition and dissemination of knowledge, and for the discovery of new knowledge, in an atmosphere of academic freedom; and in general, to secure for the people of the country all the benefits that can accrue from the acquisition and application of scientific knowledge.

Indian Parliamentary and Scientific Committee was set up in 1961 under the chairmanship of Shri Lal Bahadur Shastri, decision of the centre and the states, and the courses offered in the schools.

National Council of Educational Research and Training (NCERT) (1961) has a separate department of science education which carries the following function.

The Department of Education in Science and Mathematics (DESM) is a think-tank for Science, Mathematics and Environmental Education at the school stage and is responsible for carrying out research, development, training, evaluation and extension activities in these areas. The Department conducts experiments with teaching-learning strategies involving new methods and technologies, and develops instructional materials well as material for training of teachers and teacher-educators in Science and Mathematics for the School Community. The DESM faculty comprises experts in Physics, Chemistry, Biology, Mathematics and Environmental Education. The department undertakes curriculum development in Science and Mathematics for all school stages starting from the upper primary to the higher secondary stage. The elements of environmental education and other aspects relevant to school education are inter-woven throughout the entire school curriculum.

Another significant area of the Department's work dissemination of information in Science, Mathematics and Environmental Education through the Instructional Materials Centre of this Department and through the organisation of various activities such as Seminars, Science Exhibitions, Science Park and publication of the journal "School Seminars".

In order to strengthen Science and Mathematics education in schools, other major activities of the DESM include teacher orientation programmes, development and dissemination of popular science materials and innovative laboratory practices besides organisation of out-of-school activities in Science and Mathematics. The Department also organises the Jawaharlal Nehru National Exhibition for Science and Environmental Education for Children, which is an annual event that marks the culmination of a series of science exhibitions, organised at district, zonal and state levels. The DESM also provides academic guidance and financial support for state level exhibitions.

UNESCO Planning Mission (1963) the USSR experts of the UNESCO planning mission visited Indian on technical assistance projects. Three reports were prepared by them. These reports gave the total picture of position of science and mathematics education in India and suggested ways to improve it.

Indian Education Commission (1964-66) recommended compulsory science as part of general education and stressed that methods of teaching science should be modernised and that science teaching should be linked with agriculture and technology.

National Policy on Education (1986) has given much stress on science education and has recommended that science education should be designed to enable the learner to acquire problem solving and decision making skills as well as the ability to correlate science with health, agriculture, industry and other aspects of daily life. It has also been stressed that concerted effort be made to extend science education to all those who had to remain outside the pale of formal education.

Navodaya Vidyalayas were conceived in 1986 by Rajiv Gandhi. The scheme aims at setting up well equipped well staffed schools in rural areas, almost one in every district to provide better quality science education to the talented children.

***University Grants Commission*:** The University Grants Commission (UGC) of India is a statutory organisation set up by Union Government in 1956, for the coordination, determination and maintenance of standards of university education.

***Inter University Centres*:** One of the most innovative steps taken by the UGC for promoting excellence was the setting up of inter university centres with most modern experimental facilities or providing national facilities such as accelerators and nuclear-reactors to students and teachers from various universities.

***Institute of Technology*:** Institute of technology is a designation employed in a wide range of learning institutions awarding different types of degrees and operating often at variable levels of the educational system. It may be an institution of higher education and advanced engineering and scientific research or professional vocational education, specialising in science, engineering, and technology or different sorts of technical subjects. It may also refer to a secondary education school focused in vocational training. There are many autonomous Indian Institutes of Technology in addition to National Institutes of Technology which are Government Institutions. In addition to these, there are many other universities which offer higher technical courses. The authority over technical education in India is the AICTE.

Research in Science Education in Indian Universities

Universities are knowledge based organisations whose functions are largely confined to teaching and research. They are designed to operate to discover and disseminate knowledge by possessing significant and relevant expertise in all disciplines. India has a very vast structure of education and its higher education sector is now highly advanced, compared to its neighbouring countries. The vast network of state funded Indian universities appears to be sinking into a state, where academic performance both in teaching and research become partially marginalised. Erudition and scholarship are no longer pre-requisites for advancement through academic ranks. Research both in science and the humanities, gets back the backseat and mediocrity has become glorified. A regressive trend has been observed in the past few years in science education in universities. Science seems to be losing out to other disciplines, particularly the professional courses in attracting students. The recent trend observed in secondary and tertiary education sectors is toward non science courses. Inadequacies in the policies of the government, negligence of its importance by political parties and social organisations, etc., have accelerated the decline. The widespread impression among students is that unlike professional courses, a career in basic science is not lucrative.

Universities have long abandoned the accent on research and have become mere teaching centres. Research aptitude in students is not properly developed during their course of study. Their curriculum is neither research oriented nor updated. For many reasons majority of teachers with doctoral degrees in science are unwilling to undertake research projects or collaborative research. The academic ambience persisting in many universities do not encourage the research pursuits of faculties. Research management in universities is another very serious problem faced by many Indian universities.

Careful analysis of the situation is necessary for elucidation of this trend and finding effective strategies for strengthening science education. An extensive study was made to establish the nature of science education of the Indian universities and the current trend.

The study focused on the following topics:

- Policies and practices existing in the higher education sector.
- Analysis of the pattern of enrolment in science degree programmes in Indian universities.
- Centrally and state funded universities and their academic performance.
- Quality assessment mechanism.
- The central funding schemes in research and their distribution among universities and research institutions.

A model survey was conducted in this context to explore the mindset of the students and teachers about the issue. Students from selected colleges who study science as major was given a questionnaire for extracting their opinion towards the present system of education, the course, their aptitude towards research and similar issues. Teacher survey reflected their attitude towards teaching and research. The sample survey indicates many inadequacies at the level of teaching and learning. Remedial measures are necessary for rejuvenating the interest in science and for ensuring productivity. The conclusions made here suggest immediate action in the following areas:

- Teachers must be equipped to design the curriculum with interactive teaching component giving emphasis to research.
- Competency of the students should be measured at a collective level.
- The career in science must be made attractive.
- Support must be given to application driven research in basic science.
- Research management strategy must be strengthened.
- Teaching work and research work must be separately counted.
- Research productivity must be rewarded.
- Identification and exploitation of intellectual property right.

Long term planning and flawless polices are required to sustain the existing talent and induct new aspirants to meet the challenges of a competitive world.

19

Science Communication

For the past two decades or so, science communication activities have gained momentum in India. Efforts have been made from both governmental and nongovernmental platforms to enhance the public understanding of science. The idea is to help science and a scientific culture penetrate India's socio-culturally diverse society, and to transform it into a nation of scientifically thinking and scientifically aware people.

Historical Context

India has an impressive scientific heritage. Scientific research—in fields such as mathematics, astronomy, medicine and material science—has been carried out in the Indian sub-continent since ancient times. However, a remarkable gap has persisted between this scientific knowledge and the common man and woman and, until recently, almost no effort has been made to bridge this gap.

Throughout history, there have been attempts to take science to the common people. For example, *Vigyan* (Science)—a monthly popular science magazine in Hindi—has been published by Vigyan Parishad (a learned society of scientists and academics) since 1915.

Following Independence in 1947, the first Prime Minister of India, Pandit Jawaharlal Nehru, introduced the concept of modern 'scientific temper'—a phrase taken to mean an enquiring attitude and analytical approach that leads to national thinking and the pursuit of truth without prejudice. Accordingly, the constitution of India has a special provision "to develop the scientific temper, humanism and spirit of enquiry".

Science Communication Movement in India

After Independence, a number of government agencies and non-governmental organisations (NGOs) took their cue from the constitution and became involved in science popularisation. In this way, science communication was taken up at various levels, institutional as well as individual. Nehru was a major force behind this advancement of science in independent India.

The National Institute of Science Communication (NISCOM)—previously the Publications and Information Directorate—began publishing the Hindi popular science journal *Vigyan Pragati* (Progress in Science) in 1952. The *Science Reporter* (an English monthly) and *Science Ki Dunia* (an Urdu quarterly) followed soon after. Today, NISCOM also brings out eleven professional scientific journals and publishes various popular science books (often in Indian languages).

In 1980, science communication was given prominence in India's sixth Five Year Plan, and two years later the National Council for Science and Technology Communication (NCSTC) was established. The Council has a mandate to integrate, coordinate, catalyse and support science communication and popularisation, at the micro as well as macro level. NCSTC's programmes include training in science and technology communication, software development, research, field-based projects, and creating information networks and databases.

Other Indian government initiatives include *Vigyan Prasar*—an autonomous organisation of the Department of Science and Technology set up in 1989—which plays an important role in coordinating efforts among various scientific institutions, educational and academic bodies, laboratories, museums, industry and other organisations for the effective exchange and dissemination of scientific information. *Vigyan Prasar* also develops and disseminates software materials and organises popular science events including workshops, debates and lectures.

The National Council of Science Museums, based in Kolkata, is the coordinating body of 26 science museums and science centres across the country. Science City in Kolkata has more than 1,000 exhibits and attracts around 500,000 visitors a year. Based on the experiences and popularity of Science City, other such projects are being developed across the country.

Several NGOs have also pursued science communication programmes. The Indian Science Writers' Association (ISWA), for example, was founded in 1985 with a how to developing and nurturing the science writing profession in India. The association has around 200 members and undertakes a broad spectrum of activities including training courses, lectures and fellowships. ISWA also works with government agencies and NGOs in promoting science communication activities.

A Diversity of Science Communication Media

India's science communicators have used various modes of communication to reach out to the masses. As a result, a lot of infrastructure, software and human resources are available in the country. Each has its own significance and utility, given the vast diversities that exist in the country.

Print Media

In addition to the scientific journals (both popular and technical) published by the government, several national and regional daily newspapers have now started producing weekly science pages. In a unique initiative, Vigyan Prasar provides a weekly ready-to-print science page, in both Hindi and English, which some twenty-one newspapers use at a nominal cost.

Sadly, however, there are signs that interest in science communication is waning in the print media. For example, the Indian science magazines *Science Today* and *Bulletin of Sciences* have been discontinued, as have Indian editions of certain foreign magazines, such as *La Recherche* and *Scientific American*.

Audio-Visual Media

Variety of science-based programmes are now available on All India Radio (AIR), such as Radio-scope, Science Today, Science Magazine and Science News. In the early 1995 a landmark 144-part radio serial *Manav Ka Vikas* (Human Evolution) was jointly produced by NCSTC and AIR. The programme was broadcast simultaneously from more than eighty radio stations in eighteen Indian languages with 100,000 children and 10,000 schools registered as dedicated listeners.

A number of television channels have also been broadcasting science programmes for many years. For example, a 13-part film serial on the history of science and technology in the Indian sub-continent and its impact on the world. Entitled *Bharat Ki Chhaap*, was produced by NCSTC and broadcast on the state-run Doordarshan channel in 1989.

Folk media

As a common observation that folk media—such as puppet shows, street plays, stage performances, and folk songs and dances—successfully reach segments of society where other forms of media have limitations. These traditional means of communication have all been exploited as alternative media for science communication. They are not only entertaining, but also offer two-way communication and are cost effective.

Several voluntary agencies, such as Kerala's Shastra Sahitya Parishad (People's Science Movement), are actively involved in taking science to the people, especially through folk forms. Where print and electronic media have limits rooted in literacy levels and accessibility, folk media can play a crucial role.

'Interactive' Media

Science exhibitions, science fairs, demonstrations, seminars, workshops, lectures, scientific tours, conferences and, more recently, digital software, have the advantage of being interactive forms of science communication.

Perhaps the most impressive example is the *Vigyan Jatha*. During this massive event, science communicators march in groups from village to village, inter-acting with local people and spreading information about science relevant to their day-to-day lives. Catalysed by NCSTC, *Vigyan Jatha* could be considered the biggest science communication experiment anywhere in the world. Held in 1987 and 1992, themes have included health, water, environment, appropriate technology, superstitions, scientific thinking and literacy. Some 2,500 government agencies and NGOs have been actively involved, and the Jatha have covered nearly 40,000 locations in about 400 districts, touching almost a third of the country's population.

The annual Children's Science Congress—started in 1993 by the NCSTC Network—has become a highlight in the science communication calendar. The Congress aims to extend classroom science teaching by providing 10 to 17-year olds with an open 'laboratory' for enjoyable hands-on learning.

Another very popular and important programme in India has been the 'scientific explanation of miracles'. This programme uses trained science 'activists' to demonstrate and explain so-called miracles. In 1995, for example, the author investigated and demonstrated the phenomenon of deities drinking milk on television, and exposed it as a hoax.

Most recently, information technology has given birth to a comparatively new form of interactive science communication—digital media—which includes the Internet and CD-ROMs. This is proving to be an effective way to illustrate difficult scientific concepts. It has also made science communication more accessible both to handicapped and less education people. Through the reach of the technology is still a limiting factor, the government is working to extend this and reduce the costs of connectivity.

Present Challenges and Visions for the Future

Although much has been achieved in India, there is still an urgent need to make science communication activities more effective, both in terms of quality and quantity. We have yet to make a dent in wiping out superstitions that have prevailed throughout the ages, particularly in tribal areas where literacy levels are low and superstition is a way of life. Also, the general public is still largely ignorant about common scientific principles, such as the fact that the Earth orbits the Sun.

Mass Media

Science is not succeeding in attracting mass media interest. It rarely appears as a lead story, as editors and reporters do not consider science to be news in the normal sense. On an average, science only accounts for about three per cent of coverage by India's mass media. Additionally, readership of popular science magazines has declined—people no longer rely on print material as their only source of information.

For this reason, the Indian Science Writers Association aims to encourage the editors of newspapers and magazines to regularly feature a science column. It also hopes to increase the readership of popular science magazines, for example by making them available through digital media. In addition, publications must cater to India's many languages.

It is encouraging that radio, which is extremely popular in rural areas, has an increasing amount of scientific content. Television is following a similar pattern, with a few special channels on science and technology, and other channels featuring scientific discussions and interviews of scientists about their research. But it hasn't yet reached a satisfactory level as far as science communication is concerned.

Mass Education

There is no doubt that scientific information is becoming an essential and integral part of people's daily lives. Present and future science communication efforts have great potential in shaping the lives of the people and making their decisions more informative and rational.

However, illiteracy and ignorance are major challenges. While literacy levels are increasing (currently estimated at 52 per cent of the population), scientific literacy is still drastically low. Given India's large population, limited resources and multitude of languages, mass science education faces particularly great challenges. There have been efforts to popularise science through our eighteen regional languages, for example by producing some scientific publications in vernaculars and translating certain television and radio programmes. But without more attention on local languages, much of the population will miss out on science communication efforts.

In an ideal world science communication activities would be wide spread right down to the village level. In order to create awareness among illiterates or the newly literate–and to maintain the knowledge they acquire—folk forms must be used more frequently. In this way, superstitious beliefs could be wiped out from the society and a scientific environment is created even at the grassroots level.

Training Science Communicators

Science writing still tends to be dry and boring, making it unsurprising that few science articles interest newspapers and magazines. The number of capable science communicators and voluntary scientific organisations is alarmingly low and hardly sufficient to cater to the country's large and diverse population.

That said, a number of science communicators are being trained through postgraduate degree and diploma courses in science communication, and short-term science writing and journalism workshops. Indeed, four Indian science communicators have won UNESCO's Kalinga

Prize for their outstanding contributions to science communication and popularisation.

The way that scientific information is presented in the media needs to undergo a metamorphosis, with a new generation of the science writers and journalists presenting useful science in an interesting and innovative manner. For example, a science and technology news and features pool could be formed to allow writers and journalists to exchange information on scientific research and developments.

Networking

Most importantly, science communication activities must be conducted and governed in a systematically planned manner, under one umbrella organisation, and according to a properly defined national policy.

To an extent this issue is already being addressed. An All India People's Science network was created in the late 1980s, with 27 constituent voluntary organisation. The NCSTC Network started in 1991 with the objective of taking science popularisation activities to all the corners of the country. Presently, it has around 100 members, including NGOs and government organisations. NCSTC has also started a country wide project to compile information on science communication software, hardware, 'human ware' and agencies to facilitate further networking.

But the formation of networks of organisations alone is not sufficient. A suitable mechanism must be evolved to ensure we work together in a more cohesive manner.

We need a formal Science Media Network. In fact, moves have already been made towards a national database of science editors, writers, journalists, columnists, translators, 'scientoonists', illustrators, media-persons, producers, and media organisations interested in science coverage.

Conclusion

Following the industrial revolution in western countries, the level of science communication activities increased dramatically. In some ways, India is presently passing through a similar stage. As technology advances, the need for scientific information will also increase. Accordingly, an industrial India should soon witness a similar increase in science communication and popularisation. Indeed, the success of the information technology industry is proof of a growing scientific awareness in India.

India has undertaken a large number of science communication initiatives, and has sometimes led the way in innovative approaches. However, we should also be open to new ideas, methodologies and programmes available in other parts of the world, and similarly share with others the successful strategies we have employed.

As far as science writing and journalism are concerned, there is ample scope for furthering such efforts in developing countries. India could take the initiative in mobilising like-minded people in South Asia to form Science Writers' and Journalists' Associations in each country, ideally with help from international organisations.

The science communication scenario of our dreams is not unobtainable. Rather, it is based on technologies available today, which can be better utilised to carry scientific messages to the people. Science communication in India has a bright future.

20
Scientific Temper

"The role of scientific temper cannot be over emphasised in a country like India, where myriad dogmas and superstitions compete for one's attention. Scientific temper is an invaluable tool for the common people engaged in sound decision making not only about science but various issues of social importance. Scientific temper remains elusive even today, in spite of the fact that there is tremendous growth in science and technology and dependence on it for the growth of the country's economy. The dogmatic beliefs are being spread continually, ironically, through the means of modern science and technology. People who have vested interests in perpetuating the existing social consciousness-continue to oppose the basic tenets of scientific temper. The transition towards a society guided by the spirit of scientific enquiry will not be an easy task, it will not achieved merely by making people simply aware of the concept. It will be achieved only through democratic political process."

Nehru first defined and elaborated the concept of scientific temper in *The Discovery of India*, making the following salient points:

- There is an element of inevitability about the applications of science and technology.
- However, mere applications of science and technology will not be a sufficient condition. What is needed is 'the scientific approach, the adventurous and yet critical temper of science, the search for truth and new knowledge, the refusal to accept anything without testing and trial, the capacity to change previous conclusions in the face of new evidence, the reliance on observed fact and not on pre-conceived theory, the hard discipline of the mind—all this is necessary, not merely for the application of science but for life itself and the solution of its many problems'.
- Scientific temper is the temper of a free man.
- Scientific approach should be an integral part of our social interactions, as expressed by the quote "The scientific approach and temper are, or should be, a way of life, a process of thinking,

a method of acting and associating with life, a process of thinking, a method of acting and associating with our fellow men".

- While we live in a scientific age, there is no evidence of scientific temper in the people or their leaders.
- Even scientists who practice science do not necessarily have scientific temper.

Following Nehru's vision, the Indian Parliament adopted the Scientific Policy Resolution (SPR) of 1958, which enunciated the principles on which the growth of science and technology would be based. The SPR-1958 asserted that the Government of India visualised modern science and technology as the chief instrument for social transformation. The dominating feature of the contemporary world is the intense cultivation of science on a large scale, and its application to meet country's requirements. It is this, which, for the first time in man's history, has given to the common man in countries advanced in science, a standard of living and social and cultural amenities, which once was confined to a very small privileged minority of the population.... It is only through the scientific approach and method and the use of scientific knowledge that reasonable material and cultural amenities and services can be provided for every member of the community... (SPR, 1958).

After Nehru's death, the Congress Governments at the centre continued the legacy of Nehru. The document "Science and Technology Policy 2003 of the Government of India urges "To ensure the message of science reaches every citizen of India, men and women, young and old, so that advance scientific temper, emerge as a progressive and enlightened society, and make it possible all our people to participate fully in the development of science and technology and its application for human welfare. Indeed, science and technology will be fully integrated with all sphere national activity (Science and Technology Policy, 2003).

Following the initiative undertaken by Satish Dhawan, Abdur Rahman and P.M. Bhargava, a Society for the Promotion of Scientific Temper (SPST) was launched in 1964. Its sole objective was to promote scientific temper in the society. However, the Society did not survive long. Bhargava and Chakrabarti wrote: 'The Society for the Promotion of Scientific Temper died a natural death: this chapter on development of scientific temper in the country was closed but many lessons were learnt from it, one of them being that scientific temper was an important ingredient of any recipe for not only social and economic but also scientific and technological advancement of our country' (Bhargava and Chakrabarti, 2010:26-29). The SPST also issued a statement, which was published in *Seminar*.

Scientific temper is a way of life (defined in this context as an individual and social process of thinking and acting) which uses the scientific method and which may, consequently, include questioning, observing physical reality, testing, hypothesising, analysing, and communicating (not necessarily in that order). "Scientific temper" describes an attitude which involves the application of logic. Discussion, argument and analysis are vital parts of scientific temper.

Elements of fairness, equality and democracy are built into it. Jawaharlal Nehru was the first to use the phrase in 1946. He later gave a descriptive explanation:

> "[What is needed] is the scientific approach, the adventurous and yet critical temper of science, the search for truth and new knowledge, the refusal to accept anything without testing and trial, the capacity to change previous conclusions in the face of new evidence, the reliance on observed fact and not on pre-conceived theory, the hard discipline of the mind—all this is necessary, not merely for the application of science but for life itself and the solution of its many problems."
>
> —Jawaharlal Nehru (1946), *The Discovery of India*.

Nehru wrote that the scientific temper goes beyond the domains to which science is conventionally understood to be limited to, and deals also with the consideration of ultimate purposes, beau, goodness and truth. Nehru also contended that the scientific temper is the opposite of the method of religion, which relies on emotion and intuition and is (mis)applied "to everything in life, even to those things which are capable of intellectual inquiry and observation". While religion tends to close the mind and produce "intolerance, credulity and superstition, emotionalism and irrationalism", and "a temper of a dependent, unfree person", a scientific temper "is the temper of a free man". He also indicated that the scientific temper goes beyond objectivity and fosters creativity and progress. He envisioned that the spread of scientific temper would be accompanied by a shrinking of the domain of religion, and "the exciting adventure of fresh and never ceasing discoveries, of new panoramas opening out and new ways of living, adding to [life's] fullness and ever making it richer and more complete. Nehru states that "It is science alone that can solve the problems of hunger and poverty, of insanitation and illiteracy, of superstition and deadening custom and tradition, of vast resources running to waste, of a rich country inhabited by starving people".

The genesis and development of the idea of the scientific temper is connected to ideas expressed earlier by Charles Darwin when he said, "Freedom of thought is best promoted by the gradual illumination of men's minds, which follows from the advance of science" and by Karl Marx when he said, "Religious is the sigh of the oppressed creature, the heart of a heartless world, and the soul of soulless conditions. It is the opium of the people. The abolition of religion as the illusory happiness of the people is the demand for their real happiness. To call on them to give up their illusions about their condition is to call on them to give up a condition that requires illusion."

"To develop scientific temper, humanism and the spirit of inquiry and reform" is one of the fundamental duties of the people of the Republic of India, according to the Constitution of India.

The Government of India, though the National Council for Science and Technology Communication, dedicated the 28 February National Science Day of 2014 to the theme "Fostering Scientific Temper" to spread Nehru's vision.

The National Institute of Science Communication and Information Resources launched the scholarly serial *Journal of Scientific Temper* in 2013.

21
Technology in Education

Education technology means the use of all kinds of modern media and materials for maximising the learning experiences. Education technology is suggested by an expert as one of the potential means of impairing education effectively and efficiently. Previously, teachers used to teach in rigid, formal and stereo-typed ways. Education was then conceived as the process of transmitting knowledge and ideas. Students used to get by heart whatever was given by the teacher or textbook. They often could not understand what was taught and were expected to reproduce at the time of examination. Pupils were silent audience and could not make any logical queries or independent thinking of their own.

Today, the student is not considered as an empty vessel to be filled in by facts and figures. They are now expected to use so many media and materials and to get learning experience from all sides. Education is regarded as a process of interaction and interpersonal communication. The modern teacher has to help, to guide and facilitate the learner's development. The teacher has to inspire and motivate the young learners and assist the adult learners in their quest for knowledge and skills.

Don Knezek, the CEO of the International Society for Technology in Education, compares education without technology to the medical profession without tools. "If in 1970 you had knee surgery, you got a huge scar," he says, "Now, if you have knee surgery you have two little dots".

What is Education Technology?

Technology in education is defined as an array of tools that are helpful in advancing student learning and measured in how and why individuals behave.

Educational technology is the study and ethical practice of facilitating e-learning, which is the learning and improving performance by creating, using and managing appropriate technological processes and resources. Educational Technology relies on a broad definition of the word "technology" which significant the tools and the sources to enhanced, to develop the skill of the Education.

History of Use of Technology in Education

Educational technology could be traced back to the emergence of very early tools, e.g., paintings on cave walls. But usually its history starts with the introduction of educational films (1900s) or Sidney Presser's mechanical teaching machines in the 1920s.

The first large scale usage of new technologies can be traced to US WWII training of soldiers through training films and other mediated materials. Today, presentation-based technology, based on the idea that people can learn through aural and visual reception, exists in many forms, e.g., streaming audio and video, or PowerPoint presentations.

In the 1990s, there are a variety of schools that have Computer-based learning (CBL) system. They are frequently based on constructivist and cognitivist learning theories, these environments focused on teaching both abstract and domain-specific problem solving learning.

The 2000s emergence of multiple media and ubiquitous technologies which gave a new impulse to situated learning theories favouring learning-in-context scenarios. Students are now growing up in a digital age where they have constant exposure to a variety of media.

Why Technology is used in Education Industry?

Economists identify three factors that lead to growth which is based on increased human capacity.

- *Capital deepening*—the ability of the workforce to use equipment that is more productive than earlier versions.
- *Higher quality labour*—a more knowledgeable work force that is able to add value to economic output.
- *Technological innovation*—the ability of the workforce to create, distribute, share and use of the new knowledge.

These three productivity factors serve as the basis for three complementary, somewhat overlapping, approaches that connect education policy with economic development.

- *Technology literacy approach*—Increasing the extent to which new technology is used by students, citizens and the work force by incorporating technology skills into the school curriculum.
- *Knowledge deepening approach*—Increasing the ability of students, citizens, and the workforce to use knowledge to add value to society and the economy by applying it to solve complex, real-world problems.
- *Knowledge Creation approach*—Increasing the ability of students, citizens, and the workforce to innovate, produce new knowledge, and benefit from this new knowledge.

"Our aim was to encourage far higher levels of active student engagement, where knowledge is obtained by sharing, problem-solving and creating, rather than by passive listening. This classroom enables both active engagement and equal access" by lead researcher, Liz Burdon Britain's Durham University.

Technology as Tools of Teaching

There are various types of technologies currently used in classrooms. Among these are:

- *Computer in the classroom*: Having a computer in the classroom is an asset to any teacher. With a computer in the classroom, teachers are able to demonstrate a new lesson, present new material, illustrate how to use new programmes, and show new information on websites.
- *Class blogs and Wikipedia*: There are a variety of Web 2.0 tools that are currently being implemented in the classroom. Blogs allow for students to maintain a running dialogue, such as a journal, thoughts, ideas, and assignments that also provide for students comments and reflections. Wikipedia, an online encyclopaedia, are more group focused to allow multiple members of the group to edit a single document and create a truly collaborative and carefully edited finished product.
- *Wireless classroom microphones*: Noisy classrooms are a daily occurrence, and with the help of microphones, students are able to hear their teachers more clearly. Students learn better when they hear the teacher clearly.
- *Mobile devices*: Mobile devices such as tablet or smart phone can be used to enhance the experience in the classroom by providing the possibility for professors to get feedback.
- *Interactive whiteboards*: An interactive whiteboard that provides touch control of computer applications. These enhance the experience in the classroom by showing anything that can be on a computer screen. This not only aids in visual learning, but it is interactive so the students can draw, write, or manipulate images on the interactive whiteboard.
- *Digital video-on-demand*: Digital video eliminates the need for in-classroom hardware and allows teachers and students to access video clips immediately by not utilising the public Internet.
- *Online media*: Streamed video websites can be utilised to enhance a classroom lesson.
- *Online study tools*: Tools that motivate studying by making studying more fun or individualised for the students.

- *Digital games*: The field of educational games and serious games has been growing significantly over the last few years. The digital games are being provided as tools for the classroom and have a lot of positive feedback including higher motivation for students.

There are many other tools being utilised depending on the local school board and funds available at their disposal.

Education Technology Project in India

The Government of India in the Ministry of Education and Social Welfare realised the importance of Education Technology for Qualitative improvement of education and included the Education Technology Project in its Fifth Five-Year Plan in 1971. This project had four sub-schemes as follows:

- Setting up an Education Technology Unit in the Ministry of Education and Social Welfare.
- Establishing a Centre for Education Technology (CET) in the NCERT.
- Assisting States for setting up Education Technology Cells and their programmes on hundred per cent basis.
- Strengthening a few education institutions for undertaking Education Technology Programmes.

Accordingly, unit was started in the Ministry from 1971 and a CET in the NCERT was set-up in 1973. Education Technology Cells come into being different states from 1972-73 onwards.

The Unit in the Ministry made all planning, policy-making and providing funds for implementation of the Educational project and the CET in the NCERT started functioning in the following areas:

- Systems designing and implementation.
- Prototype production of suitable hardware and software.
- Training in different areas of Education Technology.
- Research and Evaluation.
- Collection and dissemination of information, data and consultancy services.

The Education Technology project was conceived as a broad-based and collaborative effort among the Ministry of Education and Social Welfare, the Ministry of Information and Broadcasting, the Indian Space Research Organisation and other concerned organisations. It is underlined the importance of inter-agency co-ordination, systematic planning, scientific evaluation and effective utilisation. Operationally the scheme sought to extend, the benefits of technology to large groups, particularly those in rural areas. It aimed at improving the quality of education at all levels, to reduce wastage and stagnation and to introduce new methods of teaching and innovation.

Recently, Information and Communication Technology (ICT) for education, initiative by UNESCO, conducted an extensive consultation to identify the competencies that teachers should develop to use technology effectively in the classroom. It is basically an umbrella term that encompasses all communication technologies such as internet, wireless networks, cell-phones, satellite communications, digital television computer and network hardware and software; as well as the equipment and services associated with these technologies, such as video-conferencing, e-mail and blogs, etc. that provide access to information.

Challenges of Use of Education Technology in India

Despite early implementation of technologies in Education system, India still faces teething problem for the new technologies in education. Some of them are:

- Not enough or limited access to computer hardware and computer software in education institutes.
- Lack of time in school schedule for projects involving use of technologies.
- Lack of adequate technical support for education institutes.
- Not enough teacher training opportunities are there.
- Lack of knowledge about ways to integrate technologies to enhance curriculum.
- Education technologies integration is not a priority.
- Students and teachers do not have access to the necessary technology at home.

There is also a negative facets of new technologies used in education. Many ethical questions and issues arise with this use of the latest technologies in education.

- *The copy and paste syndrome*—Schools and universities have more and more problems with students who prepare essays/project/ presentation by using material from websites or blogs. Often, students just copy pieces of information that look relevant and paste them together, without sometimes even understanding them, let alone citing them.
- *Distortion of reality*—When students are looking for some information on the website, they usually employ a search engine. This will give them a ranked list of often incredibly many search results. There is the real danger that their view of reality is distorted

by the website, by the fact that someone with enough money can influence what is written or ranked.

- *Too much trust in the information found*—When searching for some information on the website students tend to accept what they have found as true information, often without looking at other sources and hence having no justification to accept the information at face value.
- *Loss of privacy and profiling*—When students use services offered over the websites it is clear to us that they are making often information about us known to the service providers. The situation gets much more complicated if a company has a set of services so that combining all the information that potentially can be extracted gives a very detailed profile. There can be no doubt that some companies are collecting information or profiles on users, and on economic relevant developments. This may be done through stealth as described or from open social networks where many persons give away information that may well be harmful to them at some later stage.

Technology can reduce the tremendous efforts given by students to gather number of printed books and journals for acquiring knowledge and increase students' focus on more important knowledge gathering process. Equally important, technology can represent education in ways that help students understand latest concepts and ideas. The Education Technology also enables teachers to integrate project based learning. With guidance from effective teachers, students at different levels can use these tools to construct knowledge and develop skills required in modern society such as presentation skills and analytical skills.

Future of Education Technology

In the present time the teacher's role in teaching is facilitator. The teacher has to facilitate the learning by providing students with access to technology. The teachers can find the means to engage students more easily in learning and to cater to the various needs of different students.

Future of Education Technology

In India, while education technologies appears to have been taken quite seriously by many state governments and by certain private sector initiatives, most of these programmes are aimed at preparing students for the job market.

In addition, the programmes are software-centric, i.e. they emphasise the learning of a specific set of software tools. There is an urgent need to demystify this technology and de-emphasise the learning of specific tools.

A balanced generic curriculum, where computers are relegated to their due place as tools, and where they extend the horizons of other subjects is a must.

To enable technology in India, computer based learning system must be introduced from the junior level so that the students become computer savvy from very young age and are not afraid of using Education Technology when actually needed.

Educational Technology

Like any other country, the educational technology movement in India started with audio-visual aids, and teacher training institutions significantly stressed on effective use of even chalk and blackboard and later the overhead projector (OHP) (Kumar, 1996; Kulkarni, 1986). Even the beginning of the Centre for Educational Technology (renamed as the Central Institute of Educational Technology (CIET) of NCERT started as the audio-visual department of the government. So much so, the NCERT 2006 position paper of its National Focus Group (NCERT, 2006) even underlined that the stress on individualised learning in the old gurukul system can be considered as a feature of educational technology. It also notes that alternative educational technologies/instructional strategies were adopted by innovative schooling projects in the voluntary sectors such as projects on early childhood education by Badheka and Modak, Tilonia programme in Rajasthan, Kishore Bharti/Eklavya project in Hoshangabad (MP), Gram Mangal in Maharashtra, Bhandup and Avehi-Abacus projects of Mumbai municipal schools, among others.

The shift from the audio-visual movement to the programmed learning movement to the programmed learning movement (and, therefore, development of programmed learning materials—which later on led to development of training resources and self-learning materials in various sectors including distance learning) was led by Basu and Kulkarni at NCERT. That was a significant development since the audio-visual (and later the media and technology) movement needed to be balanced with the development and use of learning resources, and planning for teaching-learning guided by learning/educational objectives and mastery learning (you may like to refer to the Minimum Levels of Learning (MLL) of NCERT).

Television came to India in 1959 as a pilot project financially supported by the Ford Foundation, and the Delhi School Television Programme was initiated on 24 October 1961. However, the Satellite Instructional Television Experiment (SITE) in 1975-76 was the first interactive experiment which combined education with community participation and development. In 1974, the union government created an ET unit in the Education Ministry, the Centre for Educational Technology (CET) at NCERT, and ET cells in six site states. In 1980, when INSAT (Indian National Satellite) was launched, the Government's Doordarshan (national television) took over production and especially telecast of educational television programmes. The CIET of NCERT later started educational television programmes for school children and for primary teachers in the eighties. The GoI in collaboration with UNDP and UNESCO started INSAT for Education project; simultaneously an ET Division was established at the Ministry; the CET of NCERT was merged with its Department of Teaching Aids to be renamed as CIET; and many ET cells of state government were also renamed as State Institutes of Educational Technology. Classroom 2000+ experiment on interactive conferencing was conducted by CIET the results of which though could not be implemented widely thereafter. However, concurrently the GoI undertook a scheme of distributing radio-cum-cassette players (about 228,118) and colour TV sets (about 31,129) and using those in various schools in the country, though, the scheme also failed to integrate media and technology with classroom teaching-learning (Mukhopadhyay, *et al.*, 1993).

In so far as the computer is concerned, its experiment and use in classrooms dates back to 1984 when the CLASS (computer literature and studies) project was started as a joint venture of the Department of Electronics (DoE), GoI and NCERT. Microcomputers provided by the BBC were supplied to 2,582 schools and 42 resource centres. The experiment concluded not-so-effective use of microcomputers in teaching due largely to the gap between teacher orientation and actual use, installation other problems and lack of sufficient training. Attitude to technology was also another factor. The revised CLASS was revived during 1993-2004 with new PCs, followed by CLASS 2000 in which the government had to introduce computer literacy in 10,000 schools and computer based learning in 100 smart schools. The experience of NCERT showed that IT was not integrated into teaching-learning, rather was used as add on; and also that lack of significant policy and committed practice led to its negligence by the teachers. Subsequently, there have been a few experiments like IIT(D)-NIIT experiment on 'Hole in the Wall' computer literacy project, one-month summer course for Class V students by TeNet group of IIT (Madras), among others. A large number of urban schools today use a number of interactive multimedia CD-ROMs in the classroom, along with ETV and web resources. The use of interactive multimedia CD-ROMs on hard spots and computers was enhanced under the Computer Based Elementary Education (CBEE) of Sarva Shiksha Abhiyan (SSA) in schools in various states under a Public-Private-Partnership (PPP) model in collaboration with private IT companies, government organisation, and NGOs.

In the case of higher education, after the successful launch of INSAT-IB, the UGC initiated the UGC-INSAT Television Project (known as Countrywide Classroom-CWCR) on 15 August 1984, to produce and broadcast enrichment programmes on week days for one hour to undergraduate college students, coordinated by the Mass Communicating Cell (now Consortium for Educational Communication) of UGC, and produced by four Educational Media Research Centres and two Audio Visual Research in Universities. The Mass Communication Research Centre of Jamia Millia Islamia (now a central university) was to conduct R&D besides also producing television programmes to the related undergraduate curriculum (Panda, 1995).

Later the enrichment programmes were replaced by curriculum-based video lectures which were broadcasted and are also available at a price in the market. The UGC provided television sets and VCRs to (selected) colleges under various Five-Year Plans. Many universities, today, both teachers and students, have access to internet and web resources, online journals and books, access to the literature base of INFLIBNET, and the digital curriculum-based printed modules under the Sakshat project of MHRD, and the online video repository in engineering and technology of NPTEL (of IITs). Almost all IITs, the IIMs, the HSC, Jadavpur University, among others have developed online learning management systems (LMS) for online teaching-learning as also multimedia-based interaction through institutional network. Some also do web casting of their tele-conferencing lectures.

The use of media and technology got a wider platform after the initiation of correspondence education both at the school level and in higher education. Besides audio and video, and radio (Gyan Vani) and television (Gyan Darshan), the distance teaching institutions including the open universities and open schools also use tele-conferencing, web casting, and online platforms, IGNOU, besides all these, uses interactive radio counseling (IRC) through hits FM radio stations, mobile technology for learner support, online lecturing/ presentation through Adobe Connect, and online resource repository of digital print modules, audio and video programmes (as Open Education Resource) through its eGyankosh. The Open School system, especially the National Institute of Open Schooling, uses audio and video, radio and television, teleconferencing for teaching-learning. Besides, there is online admission, and on-demand online examination. Parallel to these media and technology deployment and use in all levels of open and distance learning, there is constant updating and diversification in course design and development models, and different styles of self-learning materials in print, audio-video, multimedia, and online LMS.

- While the use of audio, radio, video and television in teaching-learning will continue, the use of CD-ROM (multi-media) is reducing; tele-conferencing and video conferencing especially through web casting and through the 3G mobile technology (mobile phone) will increase; schools and colleges will opt for more computer-mediated communication, network/LAN based resource storage and use, use of online resource repositories, and some form of blended learning. Since there is/will be an increasing convergence of broadcasting, tele-communications, and computing, converged technologies and blended learning will continue to dominate the educational media and technology scenario in the future. In case of open learning and self learning materials (or learning resources), authentic proprietary materials will be still of value, though authentic and appropriate open education resources will be the issue to deal along with its instructional design, repurposing and copyright.

- With increasing R&D and expansion in social software, social technologies and social networking technologies, there shall be greater need for these technologies to be systematically designed within instructional design and blended learning frameworks to address diversified educational and training requirements at especially tertiary education and in cases of continuing education, lifelong learning, training, and adult education. Open software and open source social technologies will capture the mainstream, and mobile (with converged) technology will assume greater significance. Further, there shall be increasing use of ICT in adult basic education, continuing education, and lifelong learning.
- Since constructivist approaches to learning have (and shall continue to) come to the forefront of educational design and organization of teaching-learning, the future will see more of instructional systems design, instructional design, learning resources development, interaction and knowledge construction and negotiation being influenced by this. This will possibly be more in the case of online learning and training.
- Due to these development, curriculum design and selection and use of learning resources may happen in a cloud learning environment which shall provide for dynamic, 24 × 7, and customised learning design to meet the needs of individual learners. Also, there shall be more resource generation and sharing on the web through Web 2.0 and social technologies, though there shall be further questions raised about authentic resources and authentic learning, especially in the context of open education resources.

Technology in Distance Education

There has been a rapid expansion of technologies available for education and many countries are able to use these for their educational purposes. The factors that influence the fast growth of technologies include:

- The capacity, competence, flexibility and appropriateness of technologies are rapidly increasing.
- Conventional educational systems and models are slowly becoming inappropriate to meet the new challenges resulting from the explosion of new technology.
- The need for continuing education is growing—a trend that will be compounded as the population base increases.
- Increasing desire for lifelong learning opportunities at places and paces convenient to people.
- The belief and realisation that quality of learning can be greatly enhanced by the application of new technologies.
- The demand for remote and distance learners for equitable access to learning opportunities.
- In an increasingly globalised society, opportunities and occasions are emerging to work collaboratively with colleagues across the world, and
- The ability to partner with other educational institutions provides benefits economically and educationally.

We are now witnessing a major restructuring of our social, industrial and educational institutions and an increased reliance on technologies for work and education in general and distance education in particular.

Since the advent of the distance education system, developments in technology have led to four major trends:

- A wider range of media is now available for use in the home;
- There is a greater diversity of access to new media;
- The costs are coming down for new media; and
- New media are giving students greater control over their learning and greater interaction.

Various technological tools now available for distance education are:

- Audio cassettes
- Audio conferencing
- Cable TV
- Computer based audio-graphics systems
- Computer based learning
- Computer based multimedia
- Computer controlled interactive video
- Computer conferencing

- Digital video discs
- Electronic mail
- Internet
- Laser video discs
- Mobile phones
- Portals
- Remote interactive data bases
- Satellite TV
- Search engines
- Simulations
- Telephone teaching
- Teletext
- View data
- Video discs
- Video conferencing

Technologies used in distance education can be classified into three main groups—audio technologies, video technologies and computer based technologies. A further distinction is the mode of utilisation, which can be either one-way (non-interactive mode) or two-way (interactive mode). These technologies are often combined in various configurations, thus multiplying their modes of application and increasing flexibility of their utilisation.

Non-interactive and Interactive Technologies

Technology	*Non-interactive*	*Interactive*
Audio	Radio (primary carrier) Radio (subcarrier) Audio tape	Telephone Audio teleconferencing
Video	Open-broadcasting television Cable-television (one way) Videotape Instructional Television Fixed Service (TIFS) Satellite television (one-way) Slow Sam/Freeze frame television (one-way)	Microwave (point-to-point) Cable television (two-way or viewer response) Slow scan/freeze frame television (two-way) Electronic blackboard Satellite television (two-way) Video teleconferencing
Computer		Computer-assisted Instruction Computer-based Instructional Management

Selection of Valid Mix of Technologies

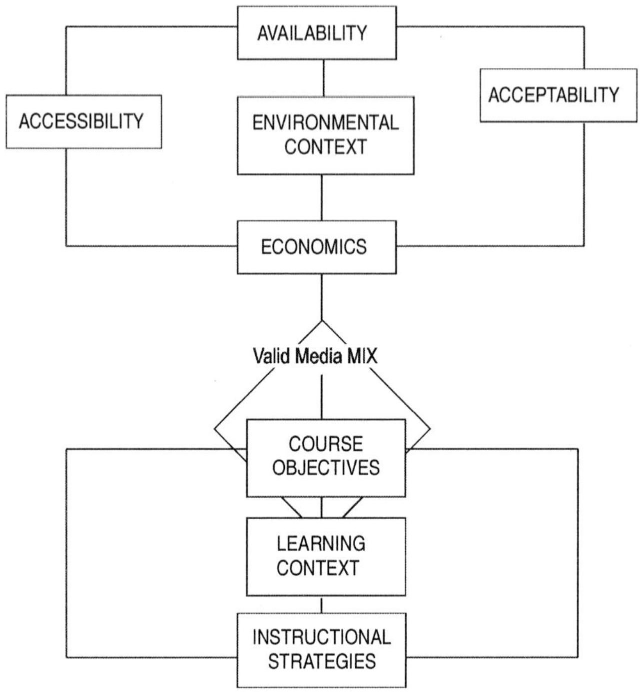

The decision to use technology, other than print, was intended to enhance the effectiveness of teaching-learning and for reaching a wider group of learner in remote rural, tribal and isolated areas.

Non-utilisation of Electronic Media

On the issue of non-utilisation at electronic media by students, experiences and opinions are collected by the researchers. The significant reasons indicated by them are the following:

1. Printed course material supplied by the University is self-sufficient and self-directing for student study.
2. Contents of electronic media programmes are already in the printed course material.
3. Electronic media programmes are not made compulsory for students by the University. Examinations do not include questions on media programmes.
4. Media programmes cover very few aspects of very few course subjects.

5. Students of regular Colleges and Universities do not use electronic media. Then why for distance students?
6. Media programme schedules are not available in advance to students.
7. Counselling sessions are held at study centres on Sundays. Some media programmes are also there on Sundays. Due to the clash, students cannot use media programmes.
8. Most of the academic counsellors and study centre Heads do not take interest in motivating students towards the use of non-print media.
9. Many first year under graduate students develop drop out tendency and are not bothered about print and non-print media.
10. Broadcast/telecast timings are not suitable to students.
11. Most of the study centres do not have proper equipment and facilities for presentation of audio and video programmes on cassettes.
12. Most of the students do not have educational media habit.
13. Most of the non-print media programmes are simple lectures and lack visuals and hence do not create appeal.
14. All radio and television broadcasts are not available at study centres on cassettes and tapes. Hence, even a small number of interested students cannot have access to media programmes.

Suggestions for Effective and Efficient Use of Technology in Distance Education

1. Induction meetings for newly admitted students every year should be held at study centres for orienting students on the usefulness of technology for student learning.
2. Student Handbooks for all courses should include advantages of print and non-print technologies to students in their learning.
3. Academic counsellors and study centre heads should motivate the students towards the use of non-print electronic media programmes.
4. All radio broadcasts and television broadcasts of the University should be put on cassettes/CDs/DVDs, and be made available to students at study centres.
5. Maximum number of study centres should be equipped with the gadgets and services necessary for presentation of electronic media programmes. In view of the increasing role of technology in distance education, the equipment needed to be placed at maximum number of study number centres of the University.
6. On Sundays and other days, study centre should conduct

additional sessions only for presentation of audio and video programmes.

7. Media production facilities at the University headquarters should be increased in terms of technical personnel and modern equipment.
8. Interaction between academics, production staff student support planners should be more and continuous.
9. Rational decision making on media components of courses should occur.

Golden Rules for Using Technology

Day-to-day technological facilities are increasing. Conscious efforts need to be made to use them in distance teaching. Bates suggests twelve golden rules for using technology in distance education:

1. Good teaching matters. Clear objectives, good structuring of learning materials, relevance to learners needs etc., apply to the use of any technology for teaching. Technology will never save bad teaching.
2. Each medium has a different range of production skills to exploit its unique features.
3. Technologies are generally flexible and interchangeable in education and training. Each technology can be used in a wide variety of ways.
4. All technologies have their strengths and weaknesses. There is no super technology.
5. All four media-print, audio, television, computer should be made available for teaching purpose in one technological form or another.
6. A limited range of technologies covering all the main media should be used.
7. Through the use of appropriate technologies, high quality interaction with learning materials and between teachers and learners can be provided.
8. The number of learners to be served over the life of a course is a critical factor in technology selection.
9. New technologies are not necessarily better for teaching than old ones.
10. Teachers should be trained to use technologies effectively.
11. Subject experts, media specialists and instructional designers are essential on every course team.
12. Concentration should be on designing the learning experience and not on testing the technology.

22
Leading Scientists

It is well established that Indian Scientists are famous around the globe. They have founded several significant scientific discoveries so far. Since the primordial period, India is considered as one of the scientific centres in the world. Thus, this country has been scientifically progressive for several centuries now and the Indian scientists have made numerous discoveries in the field of science. The various fields in which the Indian scientists have excelled include mathematics, warfare, geometry, astronomy, medicine, space science, physics, chemistry, botany.

Below there are some achievements of scientists in the arena of science and technology in India.

C.V. Raman

C.V. Raman was one of the most famous scientists of India. Raman's academic brilliance was established at a very young age. He had a pioneering work on scattering of light. C.V. Raman won the Nobel Prize for Physics in 1930. He was the first Asian and first non-White to receive any Nobel Prize in the sciences. Raman also worked on the acoustics of musical instruments. He was the first to investigate the harmonic nature of the sound of the Indian drums such as the tabla and the mridangam.

He discovered that, when light traverses a transparent material, some of the deflected light changes in wavelength. This phenomenon is now called the Raman scattering and is the result of the Raman Effect.

Prafulla Chandra Ray

He was famous academician and chemist, known for being the founder of Bengal Chemicals and Pharmaceuticals, India's first pharmaceutical company. In 1889, Prafulla Chandra was chosen an Assistant Professor of Chemistry in the Presidency College, Kolkata. His publications on miraculous nitrite and its derivatives brought him recognition from all over the world. His role as a teacher was significant as he inspired to young generation chemists in India to build up an Indian school of chemistry.

Famous Indian scientists like Meghnad Saha and Shanti Swarup Bhatnagar were among his students. Prafulla Chandra had contributed in developing industries in India. He set up the first chemical factory in India, with very minimal resources, working from his home. In 1901, this pioneering effort resulted in the formation of the Bengal Chemical and Pharmaceutical Works Ltd.

Sir Mokshagundam Visvesvaraya

He was a notable Indian engineer, scholar, statesman and the Diwan of Mysore during 1912 to 1918. Sir M. Visvesvaraya was one of the most eminent engineers of India. He maintained high principles and discipline in his life. He was best known for his contribution as the chief architect behind the construction of the Krishna Raja Sagar dam in Mandya which helped to convert the surrounding barren lands into fertile grounds for farming. Visvesvaraya was knighted as the Commander of the Order of the Indian Empire (KCIE) by the British for his contributions to the society in 1915. He was a recipient of the Indian Republic's highest honour, the Bharat Ratna for his persistent work in the fields of engineering and education. He was also awarded with several honorary doctoral degrees from universities in India.

Sir MV suggested that India try to be at par with industrialised nations as he believed that India can become developed through industries. He has the credit of inventing 'automatic sluice gates' and 'block irrigation system' which are still considered to be marvels in engineering. Each year, his birthday, 15 September, is celebrated as Engineer's Day in India.

Jagdish Chandra Bose

Jagdish Chandra Bose was eminent scientist. He developed the use of galena crystals for making receivers, both for short wavelength radio waves and for white and ultraviolet light. In 1895, two years before Marconi's demonstration, Bose demonstrated wireless communication using radio waves, using them to ring a bell remotely and to explode some gunpowder. He invented many of the microwave components such as wave guides, horn antennas, polarizers, dielectric lenses and prisms, and even semiconductor detectors of electromagnetic radiation in the last decade of the nineteenth century. He also proposed the existence of electromagnetic radiation from the Sun, which was confirmed in 1944. After that Bose focused his attention to response phenomena in plants. He presented that not only animal but vegetable tissues, produce similar electric response under different kinds of stimuli—mechanical, thermal, electrical and chemical.

Meghnad Saha

Meghnad Saha belonged to District of Dhaka, now in Bangladesh. In 1920, Meghnad Saha had developed himself as renowned physicists of the time. Meghnad Saha has contributed in the arena of the thermal ionisation of elements, and it led him to formulate what is known as the Saha Equation. This equation is one of the basic tools for interpretation of the spectra of stars in astrophysics. His theory of high-temperature ionisation of elements and its application to stellar atmospheres, as expressed by the Saha equation, is fundamental to modern astrophysics; subsequent development of his ideas has led to increased knowledge of the pressure and temperature distributions of stellar atmospheres.

By studying the spectra of various stars, one can find their temperature and from that, using Saha's equation, determine the ionisation state of the various elements making up the star. He also invented an instrument to measure the weight and pressure of solar rays. He was also the chief architect of river planning in India. He prepared the original plan for the Damodar Valley Project. He had a great role in the development of scientific institutions throughout India as well as in national economic planning involving technology.

Satyendra Nath Bose

Satyendra Nath Bose was an outstanding Indian physicist specialising in quantum mechanics. He is of course most remembered for his excellent role played in the class of particles 'bosons', which were named after him by Paul Dirac to commemorate his work in the field. Basically, he is known for his work in Quantum Physics. He is famous for "Bose-Einstein Theory" and a kind of particle in atom has been named after his name as Boson. Bose adapted a lecture at the University of Dhaka on the theory of radiation and the ultraviolet catastrophe into a short article called "Planck's Law and the Hypothesis of Light Quanta" and sent it to Albert Einstein. Einstein agreed with him, translated Bose's paper "Planck's Law and Hypothesis of Light Quanta" into German, and had it published in *Zeitschrift für Physik* under Bose's name, in 1924. This formed the basis of the Bose-Einstein Statistics. In 1937, Rabindranath Tagore dedicated his only book on science, *Visva-Parichay*, to Satyendra Nath Bose. The Government of India awarded him India's second highest civilian award, the Padma Vibhushan in 1954.

Vikram Sarabhai

Vikram Sarabhai was among distinguished scientists of India. He is considered as the Father of the Indian space programme. India's first satellite Aryabhatta launched in 1975, was one of the many projects planned by him. Like Bhabha, Sarabhai wanted the practical application of science to reach the common man. Therefore, he saw a golden opportunity to harness space science to the development of the country in the fields of communication, meteorology, remote sensing and education. The Satellite Instructional Television Experiment (SITE) launched in 1975-76, brought education to five million people in 2,400 Indian villages. In 1965, he established the Community Science Centre in Ahmedabad to popularise science among children. His profound cultural interests led him, along with his wife Mrinalini Sarabhai, to establish Darpana Academy, an institution devoted to performing arts and propagation of ancient culture of India. Besides scientist, he had a combined quality as an innovator, industrialist and visionary. He was awarded with the Bhatnagar Memorial Award for Physics in 1962, the Padma Bhushan in 1966, and was subsequently awarded the Padma Vibhushan. He was the Chairman of the Atomic Energy Commission in 1966, Vice-President and Chairman of the UN Conference on peaceful uses of outer space in 1968, and President of the 14th General Conference of the International Atomic Energy Agency. The International Astronomical Union named a crater in the moon (in the Sea of Serenity) after him, in honour of his marvellous role to science.

Anil Kakodkar

Dr. Anil Kakodkar is famous as a distinguished nuclear scientist of India. He held the post of the chairman of the Atomic Energy Commission of India (AECI) as well as the Secretary to the Government of India, Department of Atomic Energy. He received Padma Shri in 1998 and Padma Bhushan in 1999. Other awards include Hari Om Ashram Prerit Vikram Sarabhai Award (1988), H.K. Firodia Award for Excellence in Science and Technology (1997), Rockwell Medal for Excellence in Technology (1997), FICCI Award for outstanding contribution to Nuclear Science and Technology (1997-98), ANACON—1998 Life Time Achievement Award for Nuclear Sciences, Indian Science Congress Association's H.J. Bhabha Memorial Award (1999-2000), Godavari Gaurav Award (2000), Dr. Y. Nayudamma Memorial Award (2002), Chemtech Foundation's Achiever of the Year Award for Energy (2002) and Gujar Mal Modi Innovative Science and Technology Award in 2004.

A.P.J. Abdul Kalam

Dr. A.P.J. Abdul Kalam is remembered as a great scientist, an inspirational leader and an extraordinary human being. As a scientist, Kalam made an effort to develop the Polar SLV and SLV-III projects between the 1970s and 1990s. Both of which proved to be success. In the 1970s, Kalam also directed two projects, namely, Project Devil and Project Valiant, which sought to develop ballistic missiles from the technology of the successful SLV programme. Despite the disapproval of Union Cabinet, Prime Minister Indira Gandhi allotted secret funds for these aerospace projects through her discretionary powers under Kalam's directorship. Kalam played a vital role in convincing the Union Cabinet to conceal the true nature of these classified aerospace projects. His research and educational leadership brought him great laurels and prestige in 1980s, which prompted the government to initiate an advanced missile programme under his directorship.

He had brilliant and dominant personality and he was a man of vision, who always had novel ideas for the development of the country and is also popular as the 'Missile Man' of India.

Abhas Mitra

He is distinguished Indian astrophysicist and famous for his distinct views on several front-line astrophysics concepts, particularly black hole and Big Bang Cosmology. His research has received extensive attention, especially in India, which is reflected from the fact that he is one of the most frequently mentioned Indian physicists on the web. Mitra is associated with the Himalayan Gamma Ray Observatory, being set up at Han Leh jointly by Tata Institute of Fundamental Research, Bhabha Atomic Research Centre and Indian Institute of Astrophysics. He is also an Adjunct Prof. in Homi Bhabha National Science Institute since 2010. Dr. Mitra is also a member of the International Astronomical Union.

Abhay Vasant Ashtekar

He is an Indian theoretical physicist. He is the Eberly Professor of Physics and the Director of the Institute for Gravitational Physics and Geometry at Pennsylvania State University. Ashtekar created variables and he is one of the founders of loop quantum gravity and its subfield loop quantum cosmology.

Aditi Pant

She is eminent Indian oceanographer. She was a part of the Indian expedition to Antarctica in 1983 and became the first Indian woman to visit Antarctica (along with Sudipta Sengupta). Dr. Aditi was bestowed the Antarctica award with Dr. Jaya Naithani and Dr. Kanwal Vilku by the Government of India for her excellent contributions to the Antarctic programme.

Amal Kumar Raychaudhuri

He was famous Indian physicist, well-known for his research in general relativity and cosmology. His most noteworthy contribution is the eponymous Raychaudhuri equation, which demonstrates that singularities arise inevitably in general relativity and is a key ingredient in the proofs of the Penrose-Hawking singularity theorems.

Arvind Bhatnagar

He made significant contributions to Solar Astronomy, and founded several planetaria across India. He was the founder-director of the Udaipur Solar Observatory, and the founder director of Nehru Planetarium of Bombay.

Arun N. Netravali

He is an Indian-American computer engineer accredited with significant contributions in digital technology including HDTV. He conducted seminal research in digital compression, signal processing and other fields. Netravali was the ninth President of Bell Laboratories and has served as Lucent's Chief Technology Officer and Chief Network Architect. Netravali was honoured with numerous awards and honorary degrees such as the IEEE Jack S. Kilby Signal Processing Medal in 2001 (together with Thomas S. Huang), the IEEE Frederik Philips Award in 2001, the U.S. National Medal of Technology, and the Padma Bhushan from the Government of India.

Anna Mani

She was popular as an Indian physicist and meteorologist. She held the position of the Deputy Director General of the Indian Meteorological Department. She made great contributions in the field of meteorological instrumentation. She conducted research and published numerous papers on solar radiation, ozone and wind energy measurements.

Dwaram Bap Reddy

He is renowned scientist and administrator who served at the Food and Agriculture Organization of the United Nations.

Srinivasa Ramanujan

Srinivasa Ramanujan was a mathematician. He is extensively believed to be the greatest mathematician of the 20th Century. Srinivasa Ramanujan made major contribution to the analytical theory of numbers and worked on elliptic functions, continued fractions, and infinite series. His published and unpublished works have kept some of the best mathematical brains in the world.

Dr. Shanti Swarup Bhatnagar

Dr. Shanti Swaroop Bhatnagar was a notable Indian scientist. He had an interest in science and engineering during early years of life. Shanti Swarup Bhatnagar had great contribution along with Homi Bhabha, Prasanta Chandra Mahalanobis, Vikram Sarabhai and others in building post-independence Science and Technology infrastructure and in the formulation of India's science policies.

Komaravolu Chandrasekharan

He belonged to Andhra Pradesh. He attained his M.A. in Mathematics from the Presidency College, Chennai and was a Research Scholar in the Department of Mathematics of the University of Madras during 1940-1943. In 1949, he was invited by Homi Bhabha to join the School of Mathematics of the Tata Institute of Fundamental Research. With his brilliant quality as an organiser and administrator of science, he transformed the fledgling School of Mathematics of TIFR into a centre of excellence respected the world over. He initiated a very successful programme of recruitment and training of Research Scholars at TIFR. The programme continues to present day along the same principle that he set down. He put to outstanding use his contacts with the leading mathematicians of the world, encouraging many of them to visit TIFR and deliver courses of lectures over periods of two months and more. The lecture notes prepared out of these lectures and published by TIFR has great reputation in the world's mathematics community to present day. He worked in the fields of number theory and summability. His mathematical achievements are of high standard, but his contribution to Indian mathematics has been even greater.

Har Gobind Khorana

Har Gobind Khorana was an American molecular biologist of Indian origin. He was awarded the Nobel Prize in the year 1968 for his work on the interpretation of the genetic code and its function in protein synthesis. Dr. Khorana demonstrated how the genetic code determines all life processes by directing the synthesis of all cell proteins finally unravelled the secret of the DNA code of life. Dr. Khorana received numerous awards and honours such as the Novel Prize for his achievement. Distinguished Service Award, Watumull Foundation, Honolulu, Hawaii, American academy of achievement awards, Philadelphia, Pennsylvania, Padma Vibhushan, Prudential Award, J.C. Bose Medal and Willard Gibbs medal of the Chicago section of American Chemical Society. He was also elected a member of the National Academy of Sciences, Washington, as well as a Fellow of the American Association for the Advancement of Science. In 1971, he became a foreign member of USSR Academy of Sciences and in 1974, an honorary Fellow of the Indian Chemical Society.

Raja Ramanna

Dr. Raja Ramanna was a renowned physicist and nuclear scientist of India. He had a multifaceted personality and played the roles of a technologist, nuclear physicist, administrator, leader, musician, Sanskrit literature scholar, and philosophy researcher. His interest was in Nuclear Physics and particularly attention to Atomic Research and he became the head of the Bhabha Atomic Research Centre at Trombay, Bombay. Dr. Ramanna held several important positions in the course of his scientific career. These included the roles of Director in Bhabha Atomic Research Centre, Director-General in the Defence Research and Development Programme, Chairman in the Atomic Energy Commission, Vice President in Indian National Science Academy, and Director in the National Institute of Advanced Studies.

Ganapathi Thanikaimoni

He was not only involved in the study of pollen, but also made efforts to contribute to the wellbeing of the society. Thani tried his best to educate government authorities to take proper care of coastlines and to rehabilitate arid areas across India. It is well known that mangroves play a very important role in balancing the eco system; therefore Thani took steps to educate the society and the government on the necessity of mangrove. He was also one of the instigators in the UNESCO developed 'Asia and Pacific Mangrove Project'. Ganapathi Thanikaimoni's contribution to the field of pollen studies is immense and all his contribution is recorded in the book 'Palynology Manual' that was printed after his death.

Harish-Chandra

Harish Chandra was renowned Indian American mathematician and physicist who contributed fundamental work in representation theory, especially harmonic analysis on semi simple Lie groups. He was an eminent figure in the mathematics of the twentieth century. His prestigious work related to algebra, analysis, geometry, and group theory in a fundamental and epoch-making manner that consequently became the foundation on which modern work in various fields, ranging from differential geometry and mathematical physics to number theory, is being performed.

He was a member of the National Academy of Sciences of the U.S. and a Fellow of the Royal Society. Harish Chandra received many prestigious awards. He was honoured with the Cole Prize of the American Mathematical Society, in 1954. The Indian National Science Academy awarded him the Srinivasa Ramanujan Medal in 1974. In 1981, he received an honorary degree from Yale University. The Indian Government named the Harish-Chandra Research Institute, an institute devoted to Theoretical Physics and Mathematics.

G.N. Ramachandran

Gopalasamudram Narayana Iyer Ramachandran, is known for the best scientists of 20th century in India. Eminent work of G.N. Ramachandran is the Ramachandran plot, which the scientist had conceived along with Viswanathan Sasisekharan, to understand the structure of peptides. Ramachandran can be accredited for bringing together into the one field of molecular biophysics the then disparate fields of X-ray crystallography, peptide synthesis, NMR and other optical studies, and physico-chemical experimentation. In 1970, he founded the Molecular Biophysics Unit at the Indian Institute of Science which was later known as the Centre of Advanced Study in Biophysics. Ramachandran was highly honoured in India and abroad for his work. In recognising his work, most agencies in India privileged themselves and conferred a new lustre on the awards they instituted.

Prasanta Chandra Mahalanobis

He was renowned Indian scientist and applied statistician. He is best recalled for the Mahalanobis distance, a statistical measure. He made ground-breaking studies in anthropometry in India. He founded the Indian Statistical Institute, and contributed to the design of large-scale sample surveys. He developed Economic census, population census, agricultural surveys and various other large scale and in depth samples and surveys that have been esteemed around the globe. He received numerous prestigious awards that include Weldon Medal from Oxford University (1944), Fellow of the Royal Society, London (1945), President of Indian Science Congress (1950), Fellow of the Econometric Society, USA (1951), Fellow of the Pakistan Statistical Association (1952), honorary Fellow of the Royal Statistical Society, UK (1954), Sir Deviprasad Sarvadhikari Gold Medal (1957), Foreign member of the Soviet Academy of Sciences (1958), honorary Fellow of King's College, Cambridge (1959), Fellow of the American Statistical Association (1961), Durgaprasad Khaitan Gold Medal (1961), Padma Vibhushan (1968), Srinivasa Ramanujan Gold Medal (1968). Mahalanobis became the honorary President of the International Statistical Institute in 1957, and was elected a Fellow of the American Statistical Association in 1961.

Salim Ali

Dr. Salim Ali had passion to study birds in detail. He was popular as an

Indian ornithologist and naturalist. He was referred as 'birdman of India'. He became the eminent figure behind the Bombay Natural History Society after 1947 and used his personal influence to reap government support for the organisation and to create the Bharatpur bird sanctuary (Keoladeo National Park) and avert the destruction of the Silent Valley National Park. He published a research paper discussing the nature and activities of the weaver bird in 1930. The piece made him famous and established his name in the field of ornithology.

Yellapragada Subbarao

He was one of the greatest biologists of all times. He discovered the function of adenosine triphosphate as an energy source in the cell, and developed methotrexate for the treatment of cancer. Most of his career was spent in the United States. Despite A famous proverb quoted by American author, Doron K. Antrim, Yellapragada Subbarao was one of those rare people who made several significant contributions. Subbarao is also credited with the first synthesis of the chemical compounds folic acid and methotrexate. Though, Subbarao could not be awarded Nobel Prize, but his discoveries entitled him to be called as the father of targeted cancer chemotherapy.

Sam Pitroda

Satyanarayan Gangaram Pitroda generally popular as Sam Pitroda is an eminent figure. He is best known as a telecom engineer, inventor, entrepreneur and policy-maker. Pitroda founded the National Innovation Council (2010), and served as the Advisor to the Prime Minister with rank of a cabinet minister on Public Information Infrastructure and Innovation, to help democratise information. Pitroda had played immense role in developing India's foreign and domestic telecommunications policies. He is considered as well-known technical professional for the telecommunication revolution in India and specifically, the ubiquitous, yellow-signed public call offices (PCO) that quickly brought cheap and easy domestic and international public telephones all over the country.

Venkataraman Ramakrishnan

Venkataraman, Indian born American is a senior scientist in the Structural Division at the Medical Research Council Laboratory of Molecular Biology, in Cambridge, England. He has worked in various fields of biology during the earlier part of his career. He is internationally recognised for determination of atomic structure of 30s ribosomal subunit.

Ramakrishnan received numerous awards such as he was elected a Member of the European Molecular Biology Organisation (EMBO) in 2002 and a Fellow of the Royal Society (FRS) in 2003. He was chosen a Member of the US National Academy of Sciences in 2004. In 2007, Ramakrishnan was bestowed the Louis-Jeantet Prize for Medicine and the Datta Lectureship and Medal of the Federation of European Biochemical Societies (FEBS). In 2008, he won the Heatley Medal of the British Biochemical Society. Since 2008, he is a Fellow of Trinity College, Cambridge and a foreign Fellow of the Indian National Science Academy.

In 2009, Ramakrishnan was honoured with the Nobel Prize in Chemistry along with Thomas A. Steitz and Ada Yonath. He received India's second highest civilian honour, the Padma Vibhushan, in 2010. Ramakrishnan was knighted in the 2012 New Year Honours for services to Molecular Biology. In the same year, he was awarded the Sir Hans Krebs Medal by the FEBS. In 2013, he won the Spanish Jiménez-Diáz Prize. Ramakrishnan was included as one of 25 Greatest Global Living Indians by NDTV Channel, India on 14 December 2013.

Suneet Singh Tuli

He is another great scientist of India who made extraordinary contribution to enhance the position of India. Suneet Singh became popular with his innovative product that has created a history. Suneet Singh Tuli as the CEO of the company launched Aakash tablet computer which has been labelled as the world's cheapest ever tablet computer.

Vijay P. Bhatkar

Vijay Bhatkar is one of the most admired scientists and IT leaders of India. He conceptualised India's first supercomputer known as the PARAM 800 and unveiled in 1991. PARAM stood for parallel machine. Living up to its nomenclature of 'supreme', this machine, built indigenously by the Centre for Development of Advanced Computing and ranked India second after USA in the arena of supercomputing. He is credited with the creation of several national institutions, notably amongst them being C-DAC, ER&DC, IIITM-K, I2IT, ETH Research Lab, MKCL and India International Multiversity. Vijay Bhatkar is a recipient of Padma Shri and Padma Bhushan award. He was also honoured with Ramanuja Trust Award (2007), FICCI Award (1983), Petersburg Prize (2004), Priyadarshni Award (2000), National Research Development Corporation (NRDC) Award (1984–85), Gold Medal Award of Indian Geo-technical Society (1976) and Electronics Man of the Year (1992).

U.R. Rao

U.R. Rao is acclaimed as space scientist. He was former chairman of the Indian Space Research Organisation. He has developed the first satellite launched by India, Aryabhatta. It is the name given to the satellite which was an indigenously designed space-worthy satellite that set up tracking and transmitting systems in the orbital sphere. U.R. Rao, the chairman of ISRO at the time was the man behind the launch in 1975 that put India on the world map in terms of space research. He was honoured with several national and international awards.

Subhash Mukhopadhyay

He is a renowned scientist born in Kolkata, India. He made remarkable discovery in medical science. He gave life to India's first and the world's second IVF baby. The 3 October 1978 saw Subhash performing India's first 'In vitro fertilisation' which resulted in the birth of baby Durga. Tragically, Subhash was only given a posthumous recognition of his achievements in 1986 as the West Bengal Government refused to support his 'unethical' methods.

Calyampudi Radhakrishna Rao

Calyampudi Radhakrishna Rao is an Indian-born, naturalised American, mathematician and statistician. Dr. Rao is a Fellow of the Royal Society of London, and a Member of the National Academy of Sciences, USA. He was awarded the Padma Vibhushan in 2001. The C.R. Rao Award for Statistics was instituted in his honour, to be given once in two years. In 2002, he was awarded the National Medal of Science of the USA. He also received Sardar Patel Life time Achievement Award (Sardar Ratna) of the Sardar Patel Foundation India (2015), Guy Medal in Gold (2011) of the Royal Statistical Society.

Narinder Singh Kapany

He is credited for his contribution in science and acclaimed as great scientist. He had invented Fibre optics. The process to transfer information freely and almost promptly was made possible by the original work of Narinder Kapany. His research and inventions have encompassed fibre-optics communications, lasers, biomedical instrumentation, solar energy and pollution monitoring. Fibre optics have transformed the way people communicate, offering high speed data transfers as well as helping in medical procedures such as endoscopy and laser surgeries. He has multifaceted personality.

He also played significant role as an entrepreneur and business executive. Dr. Kapany has specialised in the processes of innovation and the management of technology and technology transfer. Kapany received numerous awards for his pioneering contribution in science that include 'The Excellence 2000 Award' from the USA Pan-Asian American Chamber of Commerce in 1998 and the prestigious Pravasi Bharatiya Samman, which was bestowed by the Indian government and presented by former Prime Minister Atal Bihari Vajpayee in 2004. In addition, Kapany holds over 100 patents and was a member of the National Inventors Council.

Dr. A. Sivathanu Pillai

Sivathanu Pillai is an eminent Indian scientist. He supervised the conception of indigenously developed missile systems. India's self-sustaining missile developing programme is called BrahMOS. Dr. Pillai developed the concept of the joint venture BrahMOS, which makes India one of the few countries to develop its own ballistic missiles as well as produce and supply missiles in other key areas of the world. The start of BrahMOS led to the negation of the absolute power held by Western countries.

It is documented in research reports that contemporary India has had a strong focus on science and technology, realising that it is a major element of economic development. India is among the uppermost countries in the world in the field of scientific research, positioned as one of the top five nations in the field of space exploration. The country has frequently undertaken space missions, including missions to the moon and the famed Polar Satellite Launch Vehicle (PSLV). On 16 October 2014, Indian Space Research Organisation (ISRO)'s PSLV-C26 successfully launched IRNSS-1C, the third satellite in the Indian Regional Navigation Satellite System (IRNSS), from Satish Dhawan Space Centre, Sriharikota. This is PSLV's 27th consecutive successful mission. At present, the country has a total of 17 Indian Institutes of Technology (IITs), 31 National Institutes of Technology (NITs), 677 universities awarding about 29,000 doctorate degrees, and about 40 research laboratories run by the Council of Scientific and Industrial Research (CSIR).

Indian scientists have contributed astonishingly in the growth of India. They have augmented the status of India with their scientific achievements and many of the Indian scientists have also received some prestigious international awards as well. The discoveries of the Indian scientists have been appreciated all over the world. After independence, India has accomplished several great scientific achievements. Indian scientists have showed their courage at global level and have made India one of the scientific centres of the world.

Appendix

Institutions in the Field of Science and Technology

Indian Institutes of Technology (IITs)

1. IIT Kharagpur, West Bengal
2. IIT Bombay, Maharashtra
3. IIT Kanpur, Uttar Pradesh
4. IIT Madras, Tamil Nadu
5. IIT Delhi, Delhi
6. IIT Guwahati, Assam
7. IIT Roorkee, Uttarakhand
8. IIT (BHU) Varanasi, Uttar Pradesh
9. IIT Bhubaneswar, Odisha
10. IIT Gandhinagar, Gujarat
11. IIT Hyderabad, Telangana
12. IIT Jodhpur, Rajasthan
13. IIT Patna, Bihar
14. IIT Ropar, Punjab
15. IIT Indore, Madhya Pradesh
16. IIT Mandi, Himachal Pradesh
17. IIT Palakkad, Kerala
18. IIT Tirupati, Andhra Pradesh
19. IIT Dhanbad, Jharkhand
20. IIT Bhilai, Chhattisgarh
21. IIT Goa, Goa
22. IIT Jammu, Jammu and Kashmir
23. IIT Dharwad, Karnataka

National Institutes of Technology

1. National Institute of Technology, Agartala, Tripura
2. National Institute of Technology, Patna, Bihar
3. Motilal Nehru National Institute of Technology, Allahabad, Uttar Pradesh
4. Maulana Azad National Institute of Technology, Bhopal, Madhya Pradesh
5. National Institute of Technology, Calicut, Kerala
6. National Institute of Technology, Durgapur, West Bengal
7. National Institute of Technology, Hamirpur, Himachal Pradesh
8. Malaviya National Institute of Technology, Jaipur, Rajasthan
9. Dr. B.R. Ambedkar National Institute of Technology, Jalandhar, Punjab
10. National Institute of Technology, Jamshedpur, Jharkhand
11. National Institute of Technology, Kurukshetra, Haryana
12. Visvesvaraya National Institute of Technology, Nagpur, Maharashtra
13. National Institute of Technology, Raipur, Chattisgarh
14. National Institute of Technology, Rourkela, Odisha

15. National Institute of Technology, Silchar, Assam
16. National Institute of Technology, Srinagar, Jammu & Kashmir
17. S.V. National Institute of Technology, Surat, Gujarat
18. National Institute of Technology Karnataka, Surathkal
19. National Institute of Technology, Trichy, Tamil Nadu
20. National Institute of Technology, Tadepalligudem, Andhra Pradesh
21. National Institute of Technology, Warangal, Telangana
22. National Institute of Technology, Arunachal Pradesh (Yupia)
23. National Institute of Technology, Sikkim
24. National Institute of Technology, Goa
25. National Institute of Technology, Meghalaya
26. National Institute of Technology, Nagaland
27. National Institute of Technology, Manipur
28. National Institute of Technology, Mizoram
29. National Institute of Technology, Uttarakhand
30. National Institute of Technology, Delhi
31. National Institute of Technology, Pondicherry, Puducherry

Indian Institutes of Science Education and Research

1. Indian Institutes of Science Education and Research, Pune
2. Indian Institutes of Science Education and Research, Mohali
3. Indian Institutes of Science Education and Research, Bhopal
4. Indian Institutes of Science Education and Research, Thiruvananthapuram
5. Indian Institutes of Science Education and Research, Tirupati
6. Indian Institutes of Science Education and Research, Berhampur

Defence Research and Development Organisation Cluster Centres

1. Advanced Centre for Research in High Energy Materials (ACRHEM), Hyderabad
2. Centre of Excellence in Cryptology, Kolkata
3. Centre of Millimetre Wave Semiconductor Devices and Systems, Kolkata
4. Advanced Centre for Excellence on Composite Materials (ACECM), Bengaluru
5. Research and Innovation Centre (RIC), Chennai
6. Centre of Propulsion Technology (CoPT), Mumbai
7. Jagdish Chandra Bose Centre for Advanced Technology, Jodhpur
8. Joint Advanced Technology Centre (JATC), Delhi
9. Centre of Excellence in Systems Design and Engineering, Mumbai

Defence Research and Development Organisations Labs and Establishments

1. Advanced Centre for Energetic Materials (ACEM), Nasik
2. Aeronautical Development Establishment (ADE), Bengaluru
3. Aerial Delivery Research and Development Establishment, Agra.
4. Advanced Numerical Research and Analysis Group (ANURAG), Hyderabad
5. Armament Research and Development Establishment (ARDE), Pune

6. Centre for Advanced Semiconductor Technology (ASEMIT), Delhi
7. Centre For Air Borne System (CABS), Bengaluru
8. Centre for Artificial Intelligence and Robotics (CAIR), Bengaluru
9. Centre for Military Airworthiness and Certification (CEMILAC), Bengaluru
10. Centre for Fire, Explosive and Environment Safety (CFEES), Delhi
11. Combat Vehicles Research and Development Estt. (CVRDE), Chennai
12. Defence Avionics Research Establishment (DARE), Bengaluru
13. Defence Electronics Application Laboratory (DEAL), Dehradun
14. Defence Bio-Engineering and Electro Medical Laboratory (DEBEL), Bengaluru
15. Defence Scientific Information and Documentation Centre (DESIDOC), Delhi
16. Defence Food Research Laboratory (DFRL), Mysore
17. Defence Institute of Advanced Technology (DIAT), Pune
18. Defence Institute of Bio-Energy Research (DIBER), Haldwani
19. Defence Institute of High Altitude Research (DIHAR), Leh Ladakh
20. Defence Institute of Physiology and Allied Sciences (DIPAS), Delhi
21. Defence Institute of Psychological Research (DIPR), Delhi
22. Defence Laboratory (DLJ), Jodhpur
23. Defence Electronics Research Laboratory (DLRL), Hyderabad
24. Defence Metallurgical Research Laboratory (DMRL), Hyderabad
25. Defence Materials and Stores Research and Development Establishment (DMSRDE), Kanpur
26. Defence Research and Development Establishment (DRDE), Gwalior
27. Defence Research and Development Laboratory (DRDL), Hyderabad
28. Defence Research Laboratory (DRL), Tejpur
29. Defence Terrain Research Laboratory (DTRL), Delhi
30. Gas Turbine Research Establishment (GTRE), Bangalore
31. High Energy Materials Research Laboratory (HEMRL), Pune
32. Institute of Nuclear Medicine and Allied Sciences (INMAS), Delhi
33. Instruments Research and Development Establishment (IRDE), Dehradun
34. Institute for Systems Studies and Analyses (ISSA), Delhi
35. Institute of Technology Management (ITM), Mussorie
36. Integrated Test Range (ITR), Balasore
37. Laser Science and Technology Centre (LASTEC), Delhi
38. Electronics and Radar Development Establishment (LRDE), Bengaluru
39. Microwave Tube Research and Development Centre (MTRDC), Bengaluru
40. Naval Materials Research Laboratory (NMRL), Ambernath
41. Naval Physical and Oceanographic Laboratory (NPOL), Cochin
42. Naval Science and Technological Laboratory (NSTL), Visakhapatnam
43. Proof and Experimental Establishment (PXE), Balasore
44. Research Centre Imarat (RCI), Hyderabad
45. Research and Development Establishment [RDE(E)], Pune
46. Scientific Analysis Group (SAG), Delhi
47. Snow and Avalanche Study Estt (SASE), Chandigarh
48. Solid State Physics Laboratory (SSPL), Delhi
49. Terminal Ballistics Research Laboratory (TBRL), Chandigarh
50. Vehicle Research and Development Establishment (VRDE), Ahmednagar

Engineering Institutes

State/Union Territory	*Number of Engineering Institutes*
Andaman and Nicobar Islands	1
Andhra Pradesh	825
Arunachal Pradesh	10
Assam	59
Bihar	124
Chandigarh	14
Chhattisgarh	124
Dadra and Nagar Haveli	3
Daman and Diu	2
Delhi	78
Goa	17
Gujarat	427
Haryana	416
Himachal Pradesh	64
Jammu and Kashmir	53
Jharkhand	73
Karnataka	756
Kerala	380
Madhya Pradesh	556
Maharashtra	1564
Manipur	4
Meghalaya	7
Mizoram	4
Nagaland	8
Odisha	303
Pondicherry	29
Punjab	384
Rajasthan	402
Sikkim	5
Tamil Nadu	1339
Telangana	701
Tripura	13
Uttar Pradesh	1165
Uttarakhand	197
West Bengal	286
Total	**10396**

Indian Institutes of Management

1. Indian Institutes of Management, Kolkata
2. Indian Institutes of Management, Ahmedabad

3. Indian Institutes of Management, Bengaluru
4. Indian Institutes of Management, Lucknow
5. Indian Institutes of Management, Indore
6. Indian Institutes of Management, Kozhikode
7. Indian Institutes of Management, Shillong
8. Indian Institutes of Management, Rohtak
9. Indian Institutes of Management, Ranchi
10. Indian Institutes of Management, Raipur
11. Indian Institutes of Management, Tiruchirappalli
12. Indian Institutes of Management, Kashipur
13. Indian Institutes of Management, Udaipur
14. Indian Institutes of Management, Amritsar
15. Indian Institutes of Management, Srimaur
16. Indian Institutes of Management, Sambalpur
17. Indian Institutes of Management, Visakhapatnam
18. Indian Institutes of Management, Nagpur
19. Indian Institutes of Management, Bodhgaya
20. Indian Institutes of Management, Jammu

Indian Council of Medical Research Centres

1. National Institute of Nutrition, Hyderabad (NIN), Hyderabad
2. National Centre for Laboratory Animal Science, (NCLAS), Hyderabad
3. Food and Drug Toxicology Research Centre (FDTRC), Hyderabad
4. National Animal Resource Facility for Biomedical Research, (NARFBR), Hyderabad
5. National Institute of Tuberculosis (NIRT), Chennai
6. National Institute of Epidemiology (NIE), Chennai
7. National Institute of Malaria Research, (NIMR), Delhi
8. Rejendra Memorial Research Institute of Medical Sciences, Patna
9. National Institute for Research in Reproductive Health (NIRRH), Mumbai
10. National Institute of Virology (NIV), Pune
11. Microbial Containment Complex (MCC), Pune
12. National AIDS Research Institute (NARI), Pune
13. National Institute of Occupational Health, Ahmedabad
14. National Institute of Pathology (NIP), Delhi
15. National Institute of Medical Statistics (NIMS), Delhi
16. National Institute of Cancer Prevention and Research, (NICPR-ICMR), Noida
17. Vector Control Research Centre (VCRC), Pondicherry
18. National Institute of Cholera and Enteric Diseases (NICED), Kolkata
19. National Institute for Research in Tribal Health (NIRTH), Jabalpur
20. National Institute for Disease Informatics and Research (NCDIR), Bengaluru
21. Bhopal Memorial Hospital and Research Centre (BMHRC), Bhopal
22. National Institute for Research in Environmental Health (NIREH), Bhopal
23. National JALMA Institute for Leprosy and Other Microbacterial Diseases, Agra

24. Centre for Research in Medical Entomology (CRME), Madurai
25. National Institute of Immunohaemotology (NIIH), Mumbai
26. Enterovirus Research Centre (ERC), Mumbai
27. Genetic Medicine Research Centre, Mumbai
28. Desert Medicine Research Centre (DMRC), Jodhpur
29. Regional Medical Research Centre, Port Blair
30. Regional Medical Research Centre, Bhubaneswar
31. Regional Medical Research Centre, Dibrugarh
32. Regional Medical Research Centre, Belgaum
33. ICMR, Virus Unit, Kolkata

Medical Universities

1. Pravara Institute of Medical Sciences, Ahmednagar
2. Rajasthan University of Health Sciences, Jaipur
3. Kerala University of Health Sciences, Thrissur
4. Dr. NTR University of Health Sciences, Vijayawada
5. Maharashtra University of Health Sciences, Nasik
6. The Tamil Nadu Dr. MGR Medical University, Chennai
7. West Bengal University of Health Sciences, Kolkata
8. Baba Farid University of Health Sciences, Faridkot
9. Sree Chitra Thirunal College of Engineering, Thiruvananthapuram
10. Rajiv Gandhi University of Health Sciences, Bengaluru
11. All India Institute of Medical Sciences, New Delhi
12. King George's Medical University, Lucknow
13. Jamia Hamdard, New Delhi
14. National Institute of Mental Health and Neurosciences, Bengaluru
15. Swami Rama Himalayan University, Dehradun
16. Sri Devaraj Urs Academy of Higher Education and Research, Kolar
17. Manipal Academy of Higher Education, Manipal
18. BLDE University, Bijapur
19. Sumandeep Vidyapeeth, Vadodara
20. KLE Academy of Higher Education and Research, Belgaum
21. DY Patil (Deemed to be University), Mumbai
22. Sri Balaji Vidyapeeth, Puducherry
23. Chettinad Academy of Research and Education, Kanchipuram
24. Amrita Vishwa Vidyapeeth, Coimbatore
25. Bharath Institute of Higher Education and Research, Chennai
26. Meenakshi Academy of Higher Education and Research, Chennai
27. SRM Institute of Science and Technology, Kanchipuram
28. Saveetha Institute of Medical and Technical Sciences, Chennai
29. JSS Academy of Higher Education and Research, Mysore
30. Dr. DY Patil Vidyapeeth, Pune
31. National Brain Research Centre, Gurgaon
32. Datta Meghe Institute of Management Studies, Nagpur
33. Jawaharlal Nehru Centre for Advanced Scientific Research, Bengaluru
34. National Institute of Mental Health and Neurosciences, Bengaluru
35. Yenepoya, Mangalore

36. Krishna Institute of Medical Sciences, Satara
37. Prarvara Institute of Medical Sciences, Ahmednagar
38. Sri Ramachandra Institute of Higher Education and Research, Chennai
39. Dr. MGR Educational and Research Institute, Chennai
40. Vinayaka Mission's Research Foundation, Salem
41. Santosh University, Ghaziabad
42. Institute of Liver and Billary Sciences, New Delhi
43. Bharati Vidyapeeth, Pune
44. Jamia Hamdard, New Delhi
45. Rajiv Gandhi University of Health Sciences, Bangalore
46. Baba Farid University of Health Sciences, Faridkot
47. Maharashtra University of Health Sciences, Nasik
48. Mahatma Gandhi Mission Institute of Health Sciences, Mumbai
49. Bharati Vidyapeeth, Pune
50. Manipal Academy of Higher Education, Manipal
51. Chatrapati Shahu Ji Maharaj University, Kanpur

Agricultural Universities

Central Universities

1. Banaras Hindu University, Varanasi
2. Aligarh Muslim University, Aligarh
3. Vishwa Bharti, Shantiniketan
4. Nagaland University, Medizipherma

Others

1. Dr. YSR Horticultural University, Venkataramannagudem
2. Sri Venkateswara Veterinary University, Tirupati
3. Assam Agricultural University, Jorhat
4. Bihar Agricultural University, Bhagalpur
5. Dr. Rajendra Prasad Central Agricultural University, Samstipur
6. Indira Gandhi Krishi Vishwavidyalaya, Raipur
7. Anand Agricultural University, Anand
8. Junagadh Agriculture University, Junagadh
9. Navsari Agricultural University, Navsari
10. Sardarkrushinagar Dantiwada Agricultural University, Banaskantha
11. Chaudhary Charan Singh Haryana Agricultural University, Hisar
12. Lala Lajpat Rai University of Veterinary and Animal Sciences, Hisar
13. Chaudhary Sarwan Kumar Himachal Pradesh Krishi Vishwavidyalaya, Palampur,
14. Dr. Yashwant Singh Parmar University of Horticulture and Forestry, Solan
15. Sher-e-Kashmir University of Agricultural Sciences and Technology, Jammu
16. Sher-e-Kashmir University of Agricultural Sciences and Technology, Shalimar
17. Birsa Agricultural University, Ranchi
18. Karnataka Veterinary Animal and Fisheries Sciences University, Bidar
19. University of Agricultural Sciences, Bengaluru

20. University of Agricultural Sciences, Dharwad
21. University of Agricultural Sciences, Raichur
22. University of Horticultural Sciences, Bagalkot
23. Kerala Agricultural University, Thrissur
24. Kerala University of Fisheries and Ocean Studies, Kochi
25. Kerala Veterninary and Animal Sciences University, Thiruvananthapuram
26. Jawaharlal Nehru Krishi Vishwavidyalaya, Jabalpur
27. Nanaji Deshmukh Veterinary Science University, Jabalpuur
28. Rajmata Vijayaraje Scindia Krishi Vishwa Vidyalaya, Gwalior
29. Dr. Balasheb Swant Konkan Krishi Vidyapeeth, Ratnagiri
30. Dr. Panjabrao Deshmukh Krishi Vidyapeeth, Akola
31. Maharashtra Animal and Fisheries Sciences University, Nagpur
32. Mahatma Phule Krishi Vidyapeeth, Ahmednagar
33. National Backward Krishi Vidyapeeth Solapur, Solapur
34. Vasantrao Naik Marathwada Krishi Vidyapeeth, Prabhni
35. Central Agricultural University, Imphal
36. Orissa University of Agriculture and Technology, Bhubaneswar
37. Guru Angad Dev University of Veterinary and Animal Sciences, Ludhiana
38. Punjab Agricultural University, Ludhiana
39. Agricultural University Jodhpur, Jodhpur
40. Maharana Pratap University of Agriculture and Technology, Udaipur
41. Rajasthan University of Veterinary and Animal Sciences, Bikaner
42. Sri Karan Narendra Agriculture University, Jaipur
43. Swami Keshwananad Rajasthan Agricultural University, Bikaner
44. Tamil Nadu Agricultural University, Coimbatore
45. Tamil Nadu Dr. J. Jayalalithaa Fisheries University, Nagapattinam
46. Tamil Nadu Veterinary and Animal Sciences University, Chennai
47. Banda University of Agriculture and Technology, Banda
48. Chandra Shekar Azad University of Agriculture and Technology, Kanpur
49. Narendra Deva University of Agriculture and Technology, Faizabad
50. Pandit Deen Dayal Upadhaya Pashu Chikitsa Vigyan Vishwa Vidhyalaya Evam Go Anusandhan Sansthan, Mathura
51. Rani Lakshmi Bai Central Agricultural University, Jhansi
52. Sardar Vallabh Bhai Patel University of Agriculture and Technology, Meerut
53. Govind Ballabh Pant University of Agriculture and Technology, Pantnagar
54. Veer Chandra Singh Garhwali Uttarakhand University of Horticulture and Forestry, Garhwal
55. Bidhan Chandra Krishi Viswavidyalaya, Haringhata
56. Uttar Banga Krishi Vishwavidyalaya, Cooch Behar
57. West Bengal University of Animal and Fishery Sciences, Kolkata
58. Acharya N.G. Ranga Agricultural University, Guntur

Council of Scientific and Industrial Research Laboratories

1. Advance Material and Process Research Institute, Bhopal
2. Central Building Research Institute, Roorkee
3. Centre for Cellular and Molecular Biology, Hyderabad

4. Central Drug Research Institute, Lucknow
5. Central Electro Chemical Research Institute, Karaikudi
6. Central Electronics Engineering Research Institute, Pilani
7. Central Food Technological Research Institute, Mysore
8. Central Glass and Ceramic Research Institute, Kolkata
9. Central Institute of Medicinal and Aromatic Plants, Lucknow
10. Central Institute of Mining and Fuel Research, Dhanbad
11. Central Leather Research Institute, Chennai
12. Central Mechanical Engineering Research Institute, Durgapur
13. Central Road Research Institute, New Delhi
14. Central Scientific Instruments Organisation, Chandigarh
15. Central Salt and Marine Chemicals Research Institute, Bhavnagar
16. Institute of Genomics and Integrative Biology, New Delhi
17. Institute of Himalayan Bioresource Technology, Palampur
18. Indian Institute of Chemical Biology, Kolkata
19. Indian Institute of Chemical Technology, Hyderabad
20. Indian Institute of Integrative Medicine, Jammu
21. Indian Institute of Petroleum, Dehradun
22. Indian Institute of Toxicology Research, Lucknow
23. Institute of Minerals and Materials Technology, Bhubaneswar
24. Institute of Microbial Technology, Chandigarh
25. National Aerospace Laboratories, Bangalore
26. National Botanical Research Institute, Lucknow
27. National Chemical Laboratory, Pune
28. National Environmental Engineering Research Institute, Nagpur
29. North-East Institute of Science and Technology, Jorhat
30. National Geophysical Research Institute, Hyderabad
31. National Institute of Interdisciplinary Science and Technology, Thiruvananthapuram
32. National Institute of Oceanography, Goa
33. National Institute of Science Communication and Information Resources, New Delhi
34. National Institute of Science and Technology Development Studies, New Delhi
35. National Metallurgical Laboratory, Jamshedpur
36. National Physical Laboratory, New Delhi
37. Structural Engineering Research Centre, Chennai
38. CSIR Centre for Mathematics Modelling and Computer Simulation, Bengaluru

References

Abdul Kalam, A.P.J. and Rajan, Y.S. (1998). *India: 2020*. New Delhi: Penguin Books.

Agarkar, S.C. (2017). Science Education for National Development: Indian Perspective, In: Akpan, B. (eds.) *Science Education: A Global Perspective*, Springs.

Ahmad, A. (1985). Politics of Science Policy Making in India. *Science and Public Policy*, 12(3).

Aikenhead, G.S. (2006). *Science Education for Everyday Life: Evidence-based Practice.* New York: Teachers College Press.

Atma Ram (1990). Science, Technology and Society, In: J.K. Nigam (eds.). *Indian Science:* Bose, D.N. and Subbarayana, B.V. (1971). *A Conscience History of Science in India.* New Delhi: India National Science Academy.

Bozeman, B. Slade, C.P. and Hiresh, P. (2011). Inequality in the Definition of Science and Technology Outcomes: A Conceptual Model, *Policy Sciences*, 44(3).

Chattopadhyay, D. (ed.) (1982). *Studies in the History of Science*, New Delhi: Editorial Enterprises. Congress Association.

Das, S.K. (2007). *Touching Lives. The Little Known Triumphs of the Indian Space Programme.* Delhi: Penguin Books.

Desiraju, Gautam R. (2008). Science Education and Research in India, *Economic and Political Weekly*, June 14.

Dharmpal (ed.) (1971). *Indian Science and Technology in the 18th Century: Some Contemporary European Accounts*, Delhi: Impex India.

Era of Stabilisation, New Delhi: Wiley Eastern.

Forbes, Naushad (2017). India's Innovation System: Transformed or Half Formed, In: Rakesh Mohan (ed.) *India Transformed: 25 Years of Economic Reforms*, Penguin Random House.

Garg, K.C. and Gupta, B.M. (2003). Decline in Science Education in India, *Current Science*, 84(9).

Government of India (1958). *Scientific Policy Resolution of 1958.*

Government of India (1983). *Technology Policy Statement of 1983.*

Government of India (2003). *Science and Technology of 2003.*

Government of India (2013). *Science, Technology and Innovation Policy of 2013.*

Hodson, D. (2003). Time for Action: Science Education for an Alternate Future, *International Journal of Science Education*, 25(2).

Indian National Science Academy (2001). *Pursuit and Promotion of Science: The Indian Experience*. New Delhi.

ISCA (1985). *Indira Gandhi on Science and Self-Reliance*. Kolkata: Indian Science

Kala, Land Ramdas, J. (2001). History and Philosophy of Science Cognitive Science and Science Education: Issues at the Interface, *Indian Educational Review*, 37(2).

Kana, A. (2001). *Rationale for Science, Technology and Innovation Policy.*

Kulkarni, S.S. (1986). *Introduction to Educational Technology*, New Delhi: Oxford & IBH Press.

Kumar, D. (1995). *Science and the Raj: 1857-1908*, New Delhi: OUP.

Kumar, Dr. (2012). Technology Growth in India: Some Important Concerns, *Polish Sociological Review*, 178.

Kumar, K.L. (1996). *Education Technology*, New Delhi: New Age International.

Lavkara, P.J. and Wardenburge, G. (1989). *Science Policy in International Perspectives*, London: Printer Publishers.

Lundvall, B.A. (2009). *Handbook of Innovation Systems and Developing Countries*, Chelterhan: Edward Elgar.

Madan, S., Sehgal, Y.P, and Gandhi, S.N. (2000). The out turn of Highly Qualified S&T Manpower of India, *Journal of Scientific and Industrial Research.*

Mahanti, Subodh (2013). A Perspective of Scientific Temper in India, *Journal of Scientific Temper*, 1(1).

Mashelkar, R.A. (2008). Indian Science, Technology and Society: The Changing Landscape, *Technical Society*, 30(3).

Mukhopadhyay, Ashok (2007). The Science and Technology Policy, 2003: A Critical Evaluation, *Break Through*, 12(4).

NCERT (2005). *Position Paper on Science*, New Delhi: NCERT.

Panda, S. (1990). Educational Technology and Distance Education: The Convergence and the Future, *Media and Technology for Human Resources Development*, 3(1).

Planning Commission (2006). *Report of the Steering Committee on Science and Technology*, Office of PSA to Government of India.

Power, M. (2008). The Emergence of Online Learning Environment. *MERLOT Journal of Online Learning and Teaching*, 4(4).

Rai, L.P. and Kumar, N. (2001). Structural Changes in S&T Research in India, *Scientometrics*, 50(2).

Rama Rao, P. (1997). Science and Technology from Ancient Time to Today, *Journal of Technology in Society*, 19(3).

Rao, C.N.R. (1999). Future of Science in India, *Science* (286).

Rout, Siddharth (2018). Scientific Development after Independence and its Impact on Society: A Critique on Technology Development for the Public of India. *International Journal of Advances in Social Sciences*, 6(5).

Ruivo, B. (1994). Phases and Paradigms of Science Policy? *Science and Public Policy*, 21(3).

Sanker, U. (2007). *The Economics of India's Space Programme*, New Delhi: Oxford Science and Technology Policy, 2003. *Current Science*, 84(1).

Sethi, H. (1988). The Great Technology Run, *Economic and Political Weekly*, May 14, 1999.

Sharma, Dhirendra (1976). Growth and Failures of India's Science Policy, *Economic and Political Weekly*, 11(51).

Sharma, R.C. (1975). *Modern, Sciences Teaching*. Delhi: Dhanputra and Sons.

Shukle, R. (2005). *India Science Report: Science Education, Human Resources and Public Attitude towards Science and Technology*. New Delhi: NCAER.

Singh, Baldev (1986). *Jawaharlal Nehru on Science*. New Delhi: Nehru Memorial and Library.

Sivaram, C. (2002). The Genesis of CSIR, *Resources*, 7(4).

Subodh, Mahanti (2013). *A Perspective on Scientific Temper in India*, 1(1).

Thakur, B., Gupta, R., and Singh, R. (2012). Changing Face of India's Industrial Policies: A Look, *International Journal of Scientific and Research Publications*, 2(12).

The Hindu (2003). Showcasing the CSIR, 8 May 2003.

UNESCO (2007). *Asia Pacific Perspectives on Ethics of Science and Technology*, UNESCO Asia and Pacific Regional Bureau of Education, Bangkok.

Wardenburge, G. (1989) Kumar, D. (1995). *Science and the Raj: 1857–1908*, New Delhi: OUP.

Woodhouse, E. and Sarewat, D. (2007). Science Policies for Reducing Social Inequalities. *Science Public Policy*, 34(2).

Xila, Yu (ed.) (2017). *China's Rise as a Major Contribute to Science and Technology. Proceedings of the National Academy of Sciences.*

Index